For Maria Angelina

PETER ZUMTHOR
1990–1997

Buildings and Projects
Volume 2

Edited by Thomas Durisch

Scheidegger & Spiess

Volume 1   1985–1989

What I Do

Atelier Zumthor, Haldenstein, Graubünden
Shelter for Roman Archaeological Ruins, Chur, Graubünden
Caplutta Sogn Benedetg, Sumvitg, Graubünden
Spittelhof Housing Complex, Biel-Benken near Basel
Rindermarkt Apartment Building, Zurich
Rothorn Gondola Station, Valbella, Graubünden
Apartments for Senior Citizens, Masans, Chur, Graubünden
Bregenz Art Museum, Austria

Volume 2   1990–1997

Gugalun House, Versam, Graubünden	7
Therme Vals, Graubünden	23
Topography of Terror, Berlin, Germany	57
Herz Jesu Church, Munich, Germany	81
Laban Centre for Movement and Dance, London, England	91
Swiss Sound Box, Expo 2000, Hanover, Germany	103
Luzi House, Jenaz, Graubünden	123
Kolumba Art Museum, Cologne, Germany	145

Volume 3   1998–2001

Poetic Landscape, Bad Salzuflen, Germany
Zumthor House, Haldenstein, Graubünden
Mountain Hotel, Tschlin, Graubünden
I Ching Gallery, Dia Center for the Arts, Beacon, New York, USA
Harjunkulma Apartment Building, Jyväskylä, Finland
Pingus Winery, Valbuena de Duero, Spain
Bruder Klaus Field Chapel, Wachendorf, Germany
Additional Cabins, Pension Briol, Barbian-Dreikirchen, Italy

Volume 4   2002–2007

Galerie Bastian, Berlin, Germany
Redevelopment of De Meelfabriek, Leiden, Holland
Summer Restaurant Insel Ufnau, Lake Zurich
Corporate Learning Center, Aabach Estate, Risch, Zug
Almannajuvet Zinc Mine Museum, Sauda, Norway
Güterareal Residential Development, Lucerne
A Tower for Therme Vals, Graubünden
Leis Houses, Oberhus and Unterhus, Vals, Graubünden
Hisham's Palace, Jericho, Palestinian Territories
Steilneset Memorial, Vardø, Norway

Volume 5   2008–2013

Nomads of Atacama Hotel, San Pedro de Atacama, Chile
Bregenzerwald House of Craftsmanship, Andelsbuch, Austria
Chivelstone House, Devon, England
Los Angeles County Museum of Art, LACMA, California, USA
New City Gate with Theater and Café, Isny im Allgäu, Germany
Adaptable Theater for Riom Castle, Riom, Graubünden
House of Seven Gardens, Doha, Qatar
Serpentine Gallery Pavilion, London, England
Perm State Art Gallery, Perm, Russia

List of Works 1968–2013
Texts by Peter Zumthor
Biography
Collaborators 1985–2013
The Work of Many
Acknowledgments
Picture Credits

Gugalun House, Versam, Graubünden
1990–1994

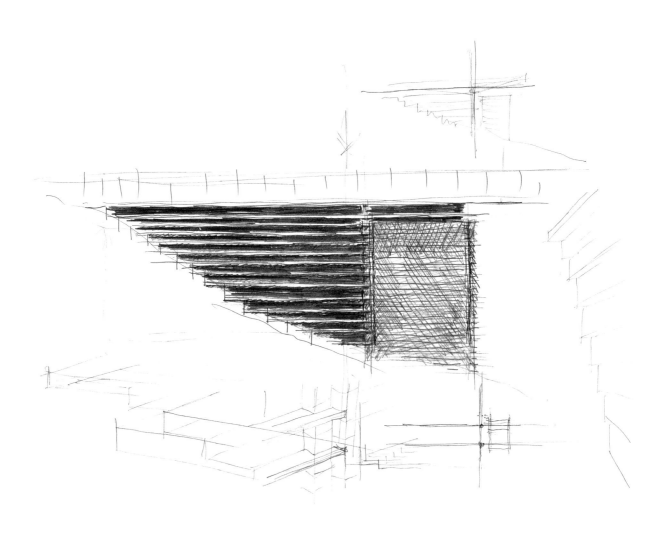

Our theme was Old and New. A simple, seventeenth-century farmhouse that faces north and looks at the moon, as its name "Gugalun" says, was to have a new addition with bathroom, kitchen, heating, and two bedrooms—an important modernization for the continued life of this modest old farmstead. A new roof would shelter and connect the old and the new.

The walls for the addition on the slope side of the house are made of thermally insulated wooden box girder joists, which we developed for this application. The construction allowed a seamless connection between the historical house and the new addition, and the stepped concrete foundation provided a logical response to the upward slope.

The feel of the interior spaces is intimate and modest, but atmospherically dense. In the center of the new portion of the house, as part of its supporting structure, we constructed a monolith of dark, gleaming concrete, in which we left hollow recesses. In winter warm air from the built-in wood stove in the kitchen flows through these hollow spaces. The old section of the house, with its little parlor, side room, and the bedrooms with their tiny windows from olden times, has kept its secret.

HAUS TRUOG GUGALUN 7104 VERSAM
WESTFASSADE   MST. 1:20

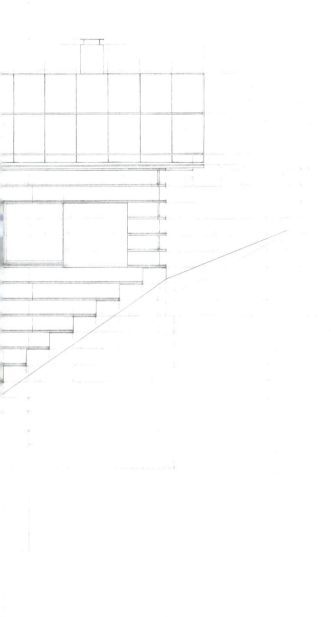

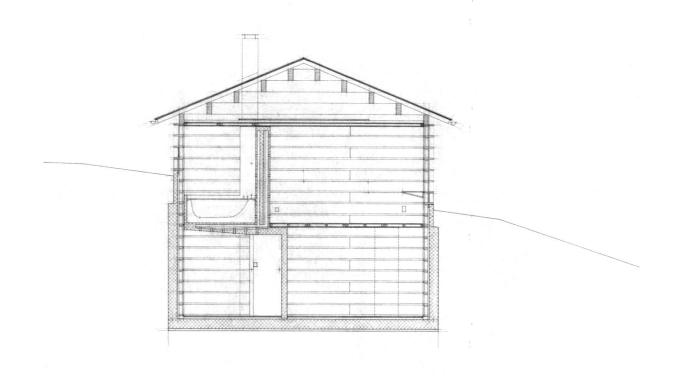
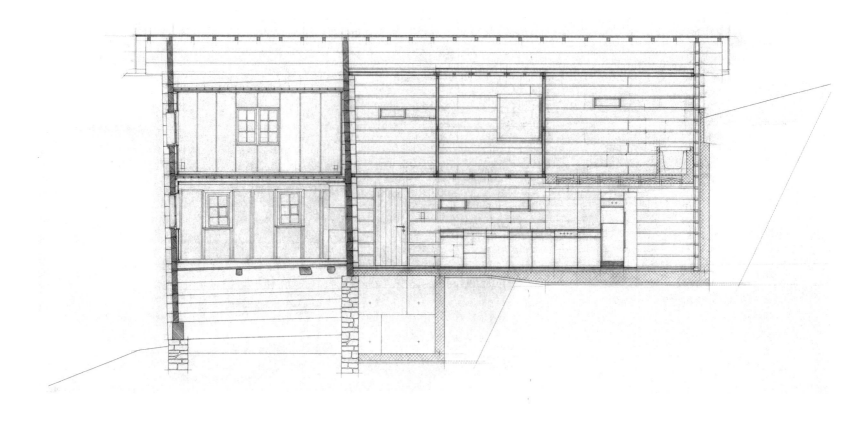

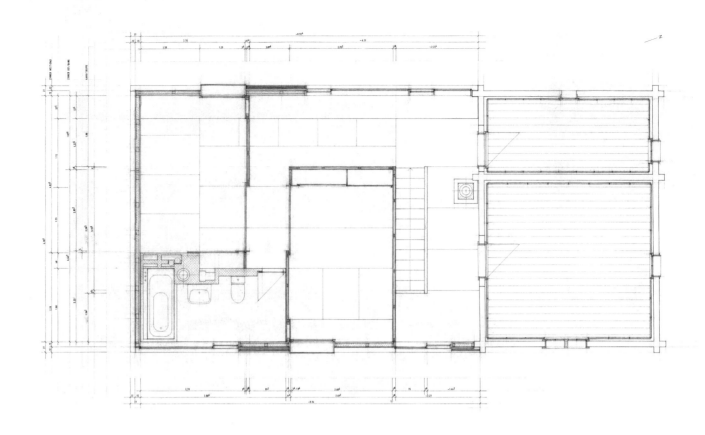
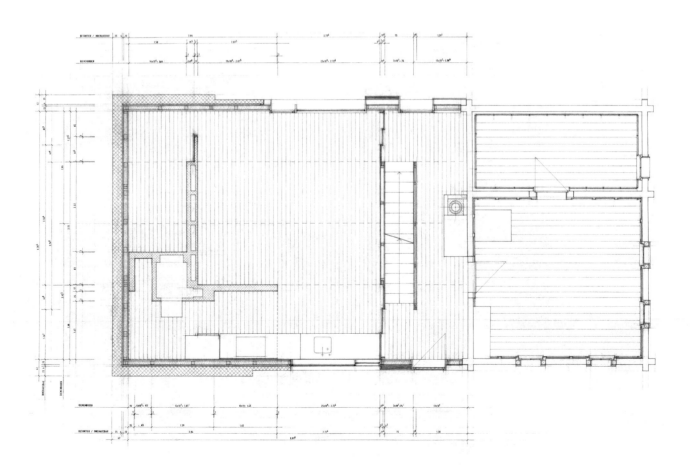

Therme Vals, Graubünden
1990–1996

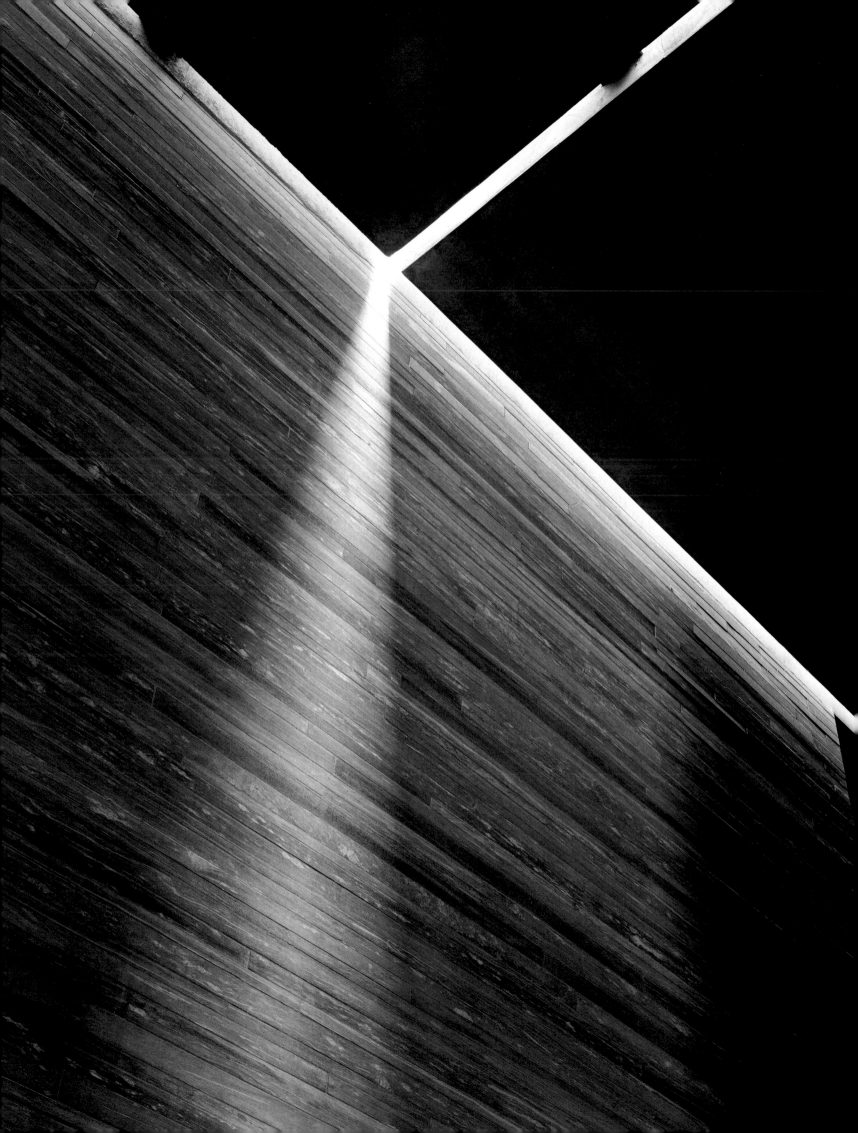

Stone and water: a love affair. At some point in the design process it was no longer difficult to grasp these two primary materials as mutually invigorating energies, and to trust that with this pair of elements we could create and express almost everything that our thermal spa in the mountains seemed to require.

The stones come from the local quarry in Vals, located a few hundred meters further back in the valley. As the stone is pliable and contains quartz, we sliced it into long thin slabs and stacked them up into large monolithic blocks. An early draft shows great blocks of stone in the water as if they were in a flooded quarry.

Stone is everywhere in Vals, and the presence of water is powerful. Eighty-four-degree water flows out of the hillside directly behind the new thermal bath. There it is collected and channeled into the different pools of the spa, where it is heated up to one-hundred-and-eight degrees, cooled down with the addition of fresh water to fifty-seven degrees, or converted to steam for the steam bath. Users enjoy the water not only at various temperatures but in different spaces and conditions: in bright light, darkness, and twilight, or standing in shadow and looking into the brightness of a colorful, illuminated landscape. Sunlight trickles in through narrow slits or through the gaps we left open between the stone slabs of the ceiling. Daylight and landscape images flood the giant windows, giving shape and texture to the surfaces of stone and water in the changing light of the days and seasons.

What is here described so easily, as if conceiving and creating a thermal spa were the most natural thing in the world, is in fact the product of prolonged study. The first spa we designed in the late nineteen-eighties as part of a new hotel project put out for bid by the town of Vals was a conventional indoor pool in classic modernist style, placed deep inside the new hotel we were proposing. Only later did we start to see Vals in a new light, suddenly noticing the topography, the rock faces, the stones, the water, until our initial architectural models became less and less relevant. But we were still working with two or three different kinds of stone and a palette of additional materials and colors; then, in the end, we settled on a single kind of rock: the indigenous gneiss of Vals. We placed our trust in the local resources, and in the energies of the people there, and all at once there was this sense of creating something prehistoric, and we discovered that, without meaning to, we had arrived at the classical Roman and Oriental bathing cultures, and the pleasures and rituals of cleansing the body in water. The sport swimming pool and pool complex with its slides and artificial whirlpools, still being built everywhere back then, had faded far into the background.

Our client was the village of Vals, owner of the spa and hotel. The small mountain community was able to commission a building on this scale because of revenues in the form of water taxes, generated for the community by the Zervreila reservoir and hydroelectric dam that had been built further back in the valley in the nineteen-fifties. Working together over several years with village men to design and construct something that was beyond the established models and standardized details of the time in retrospect seems to be a fluke of history. The collaboration was marked by much healthy common sense, self-confidence, and enthusiasm. External marketing advisors repeatedly saw this as dangerous naiveté and predicted disaster. But no sooner was the project completed than the baths became popular with the general public and a financial success. The "spring" of its architectural uniqueness lies in our having rejected the goal of a low-risk mainstream concept as suggested by market-oriented project developers and instead inventing something brand new that emerges out of the place itself.

I described in detail the rules and standards we developed for the conceptualization and construction of the spa in the book *Therme Vals* (Zurich, 2007). Sensuous images of the physical experience of stone and water and light, translated into geometry and space and construction, inspired our work.

The design from inside to outside was central to the concept. We dreamed of a kaleidoscope of room sequences, affording ever new experiences—to the ambling, curious, astonished, or surprised visitor. Like walking in a forest without a path. A feeling of freedom, the pleasure of discovery.

The principle of confined movement in a few places and then expansive freedom of movement in larger areas inside the building is something I discovered while working on the Therme Vals and have subsequently used again and again. At the Swiss Pavilion for Expo 2000 in Hanover, the unhindered freedom of the visitors to wander about was crucial to the spatial experience of the architectural structure.

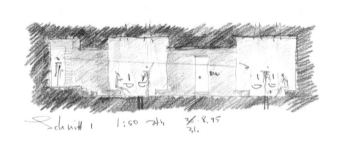
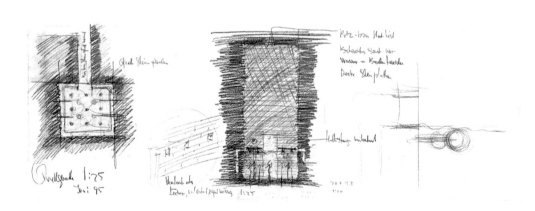

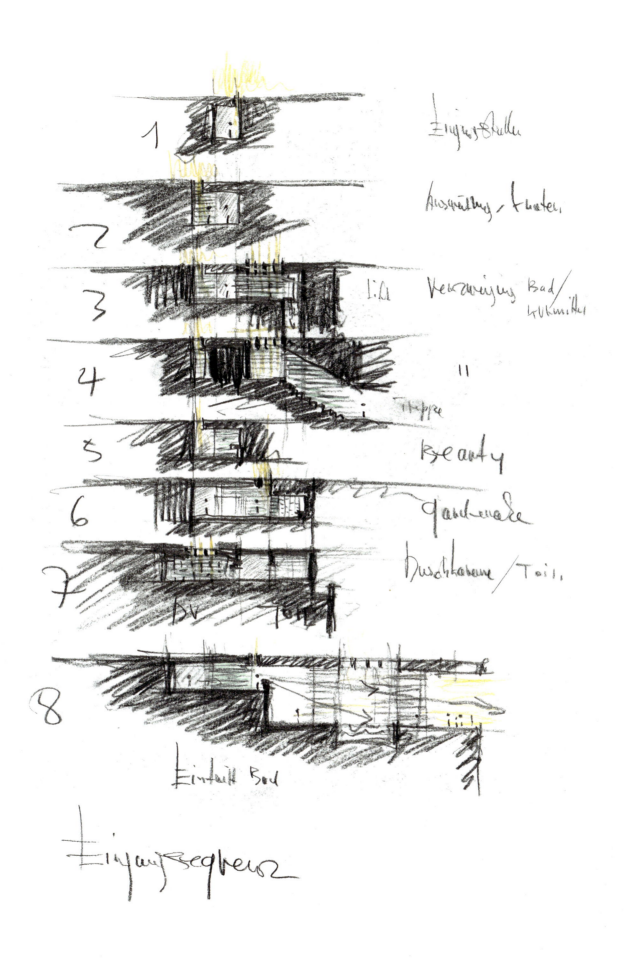

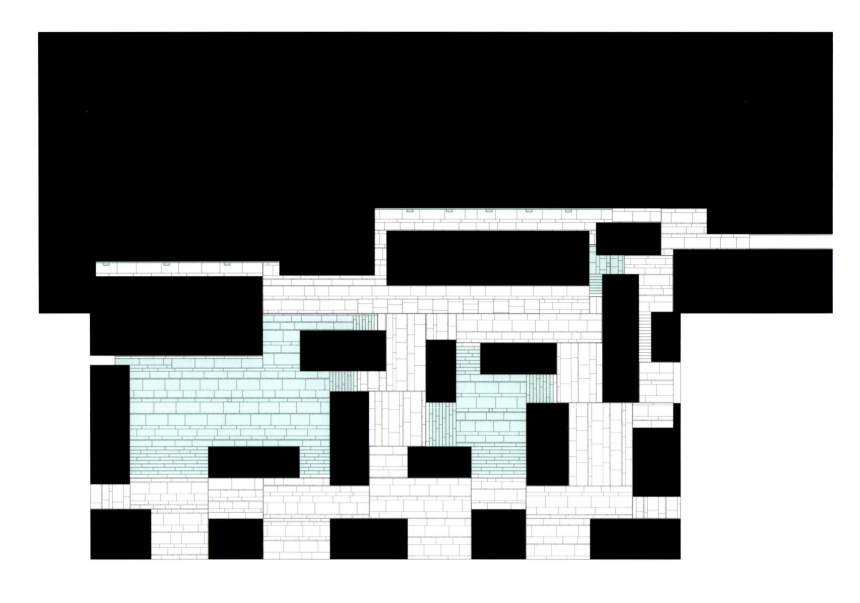
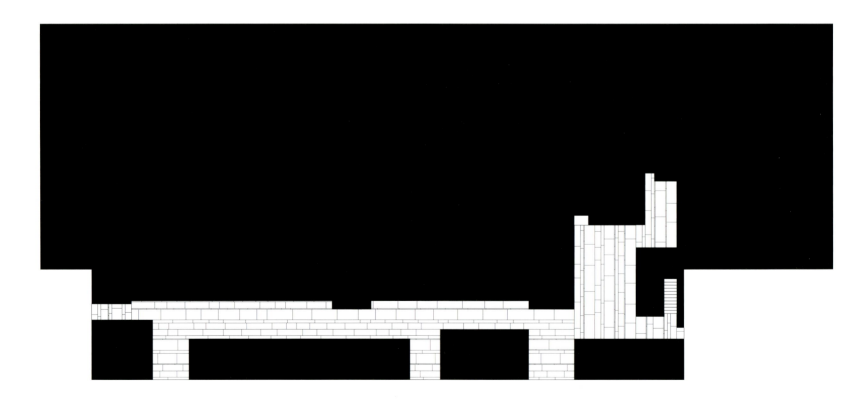

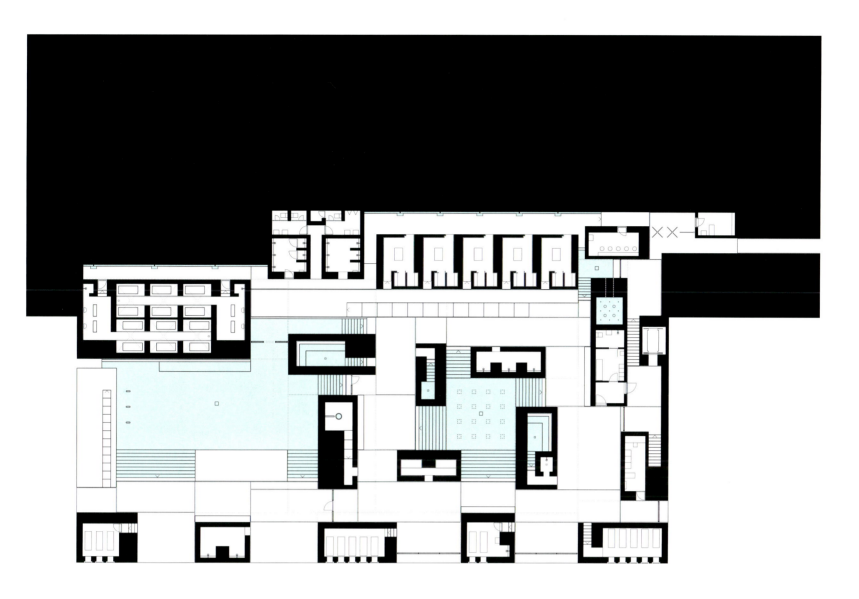

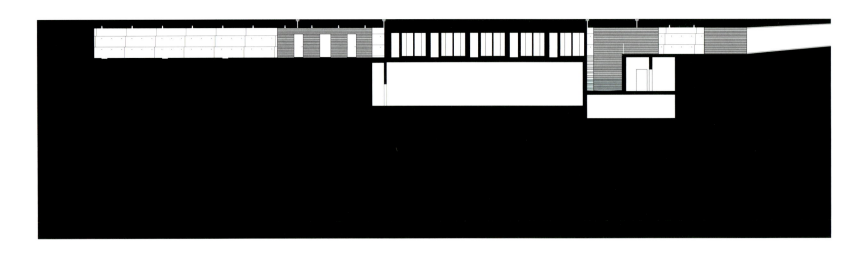
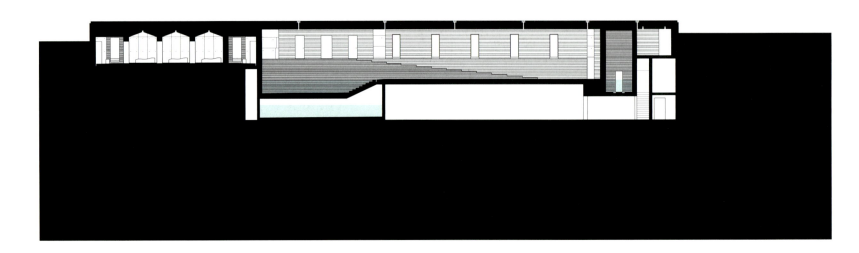

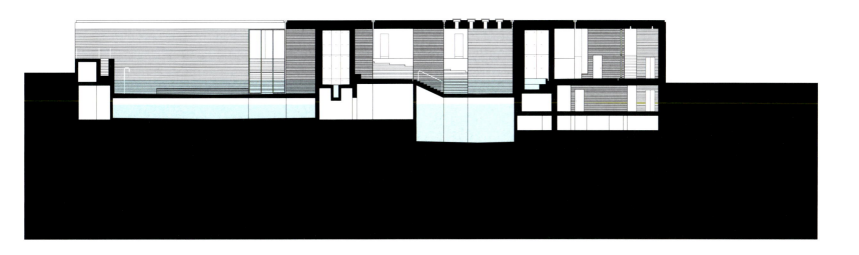
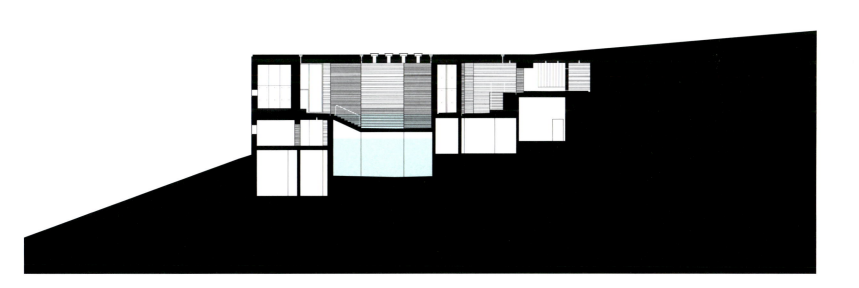

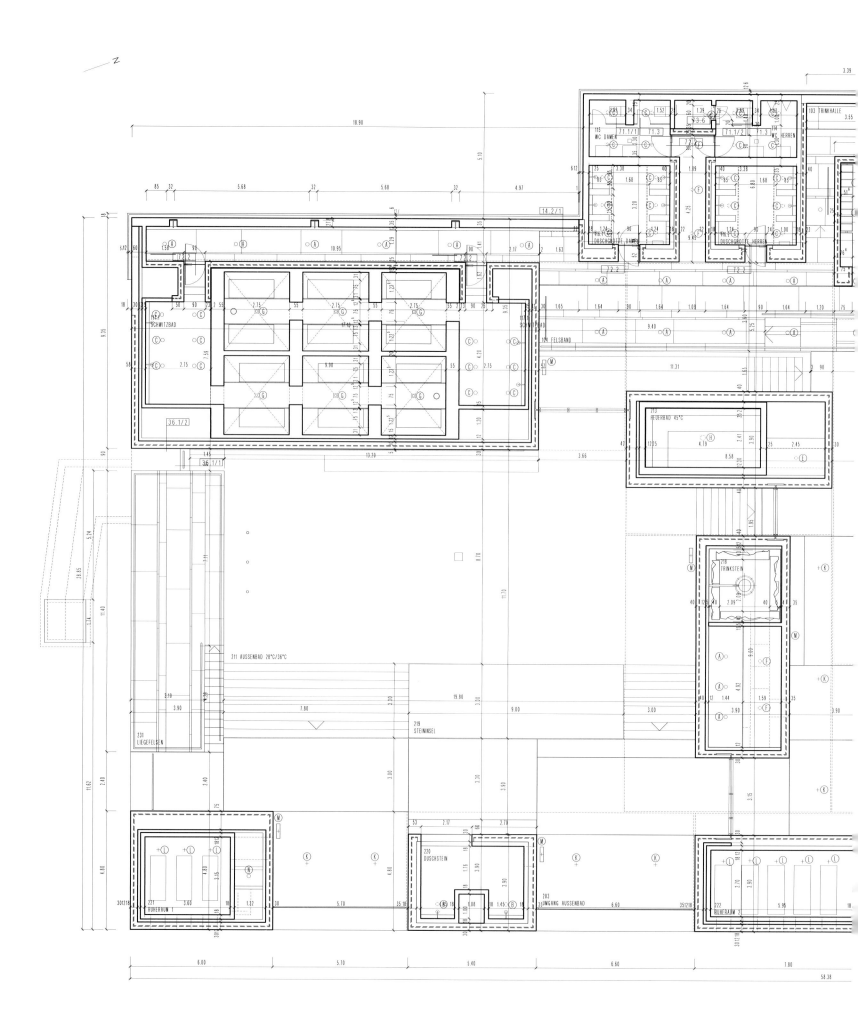

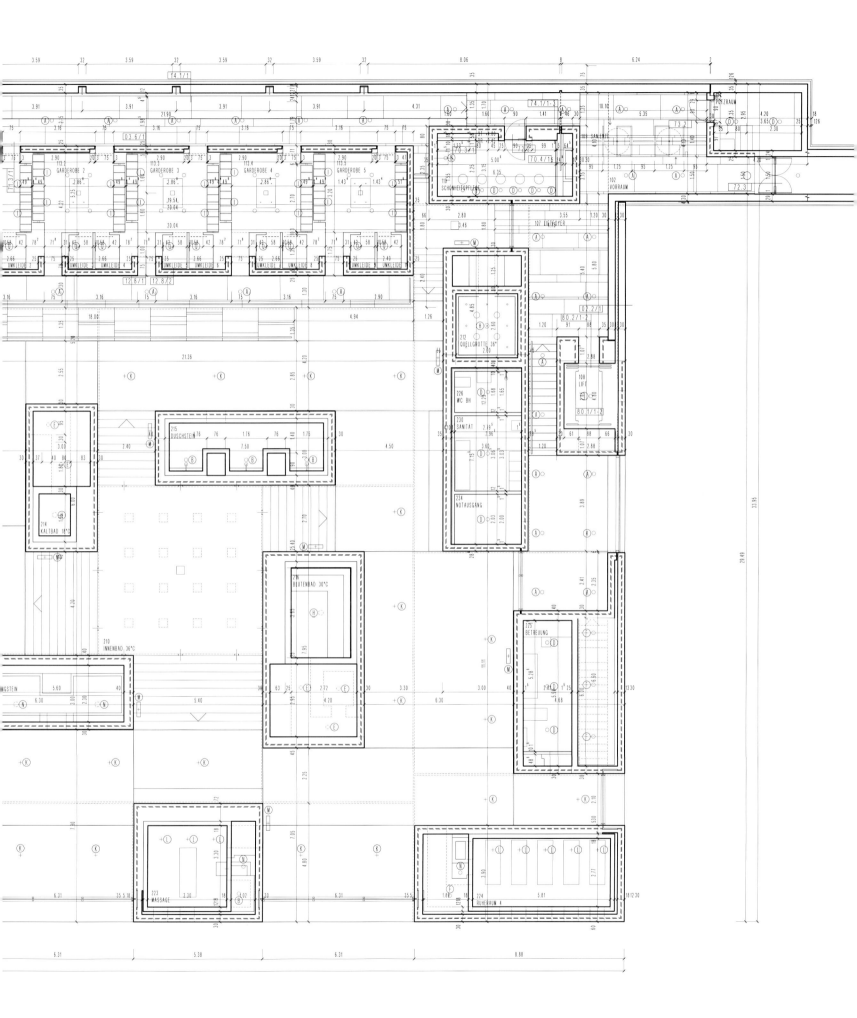

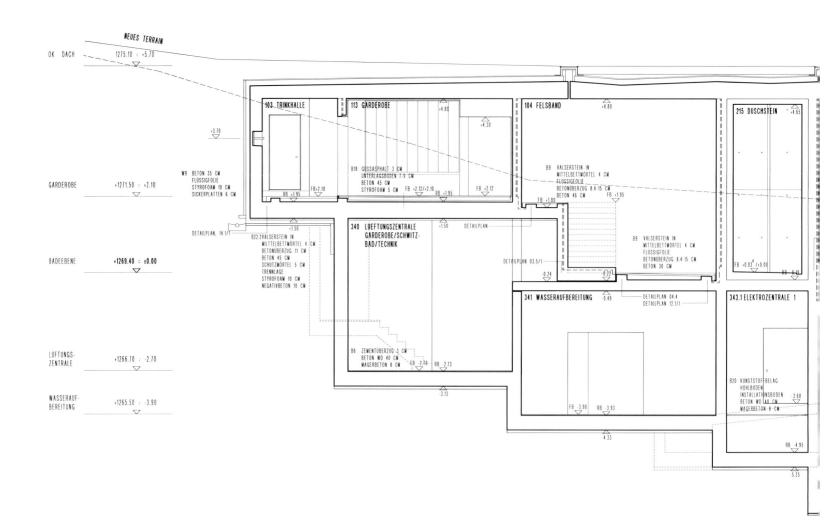

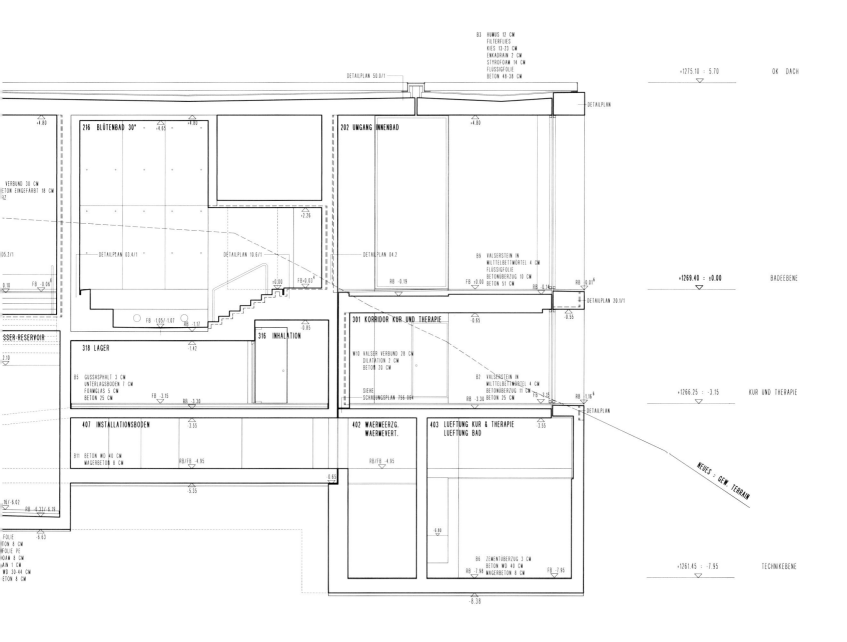

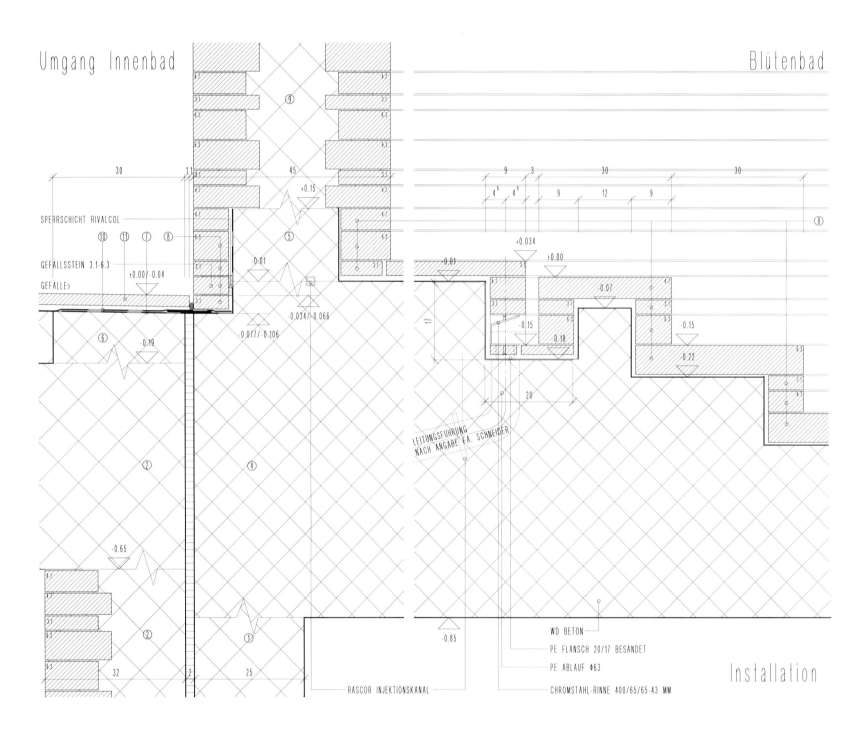

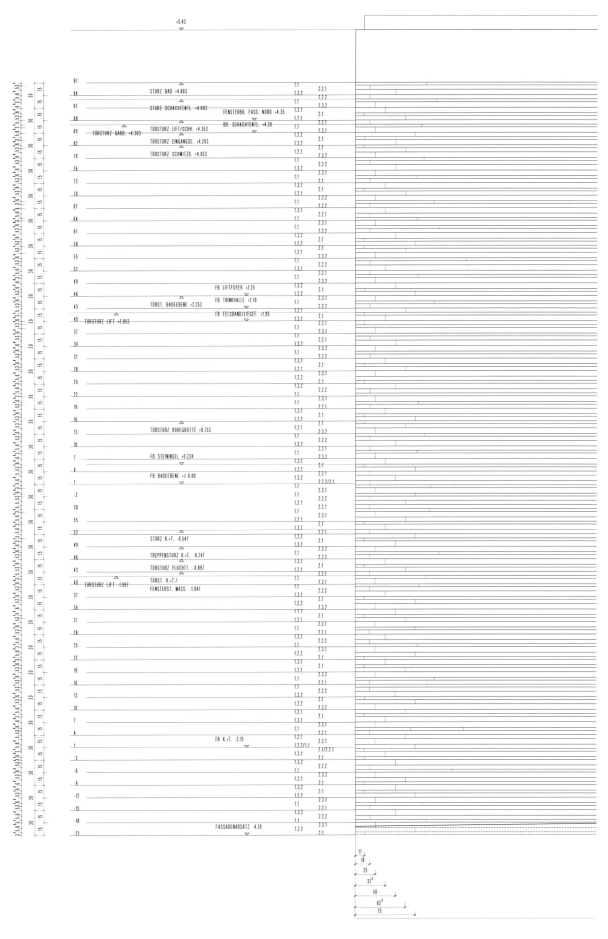

SCHICHTENFOLGE (GANZES BAD)
SCHICHT NR.

STEINTYPEN (IM ECKVERBAND)

Topography of Terror, International Exhibition and
Documentation Center, Berlin, Germany
1993–2004

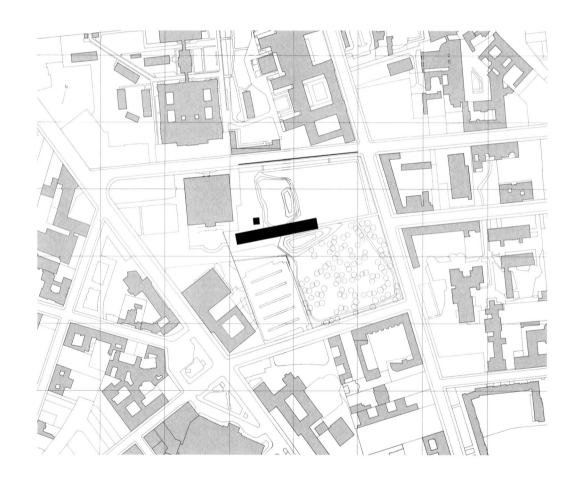

The international exhibition and documentation center "Topography of Terror" was to become a building for which there were no precedents. It was to use the site of the former Gestapo headquarters, the SS leadership, the Security Service (Sicherheitsdienst) branch of the SS, and the main office for Reich security, located during the Third Reich on Prinz-Albrecht-Strasse, now Niederkirchnerstrasse. We designed the building to remember the crimes planned and carried out there.

We wanted to let this historic terrain speak for itself, and to preserve and display those few remaining vestiges of the National Socialist buildings and grounds which escaped the thorough rubble clearance ordered for the site after the war. When we started working on the design we felt that there basically cannot be a form (or at least no previously known form) for a building on a site where crimes against humanity were planned and perpetrated. So we looked for a new form, and invented the bar structure, a building that aims to be pure construction and that is unlike any other building.

This bar structure consists of concrete staves laid over each other in a crisscross pattern, and joined at the point of intersection to produce rigid frames, so-called Vierendeel trusses. The systematic arrangement of these frames in various forms creates the different spaces of the building. It is all statics, engineering, structure. The intervals between the staves are glazed. The building stands on its terrain lightly, diaphanously. It is all transparent.

The bar structure of our building was not meant to symbolize anything. It was supposed to be just itself, a transparent shell, concealing nothing and in this way contributing to keeping open an important site of National Socialist history, which had already been more than half filled in and "civilized." We did not want to change this barren open landscape containing only two piles of rubble and a few ruins as a reminder of its appalling history; we wanted to let the postwar presence of the place speak for itself. On the actual terrain of the site and without comment, therefore, we wanted to display only those historical documents that have an immediate connection to the place. This also applies to the ground floor of the new building, which was conceived of as a transparent shell for the basement that housed the kitchen used by the Nazis, and to the adjoining exhibition space, as this ground-level space was meant to be perceived as a part of the terrain. We dedicated the two upper stories of the building to its historical placement and documentation, its role in writing history, to teaching, interpretation, and information.

We encountered little appreciation in Berlin for this approach to the site. At the start of construction, without our knowledge, workers hauled away the two rubble mounds, which along with the elongated building were integral to the shape of our design. The users of our building, the historians of the Topography of Terror Foundation, did not think much of our concept of separating facts from commentary, of first letting the place speak for itself, and concentrating the historical treatment on the upper levels of the building.

These and other objections to our project were raised right after the competition in 1993. There was also a group of memory theoreticians who wanted the new building to play only a service role, and who in an allusion to Robert Venturi's idea of the "decorated shed" wanted to have the museum take the form of an "undecorated shed." It soon turned out that the Berlin building authority had budgeted far too little for a construction of the desired size. The overall financial situation of the project deteriorated when the State of Berlin had a temporary budget freeze and could no longer pay the project planners. Later the framing work was put out for bid and awarded to a Berlin construction company which was unable to carry out the work. It had received the contract award amid the competitive pressure of the bidding and the budgetary constraints of the Berlin building authority, and very soon found itself incapable of building the bar structure for the price offered. The contractor had not taken at face value the explicitly delineated qualitative requirements involved in the bar structure. From that point on the project was bad-mouthed by the media and presented as unbuildable. In 2004, just before the Berlin building authority had planned to resume construction, the project was abandoned, despite its well-conceived engineering. The project directors in the municipal building administration, who some time earlier had managed to obtain a new, barely adequate budget from the state authorities, were surprised by this decision, as were we architects. The decision not to go ahead with the building was the result of political machinations by the Federal Government. The foundations, basement rooms, and stair towers put in seven years earlier were torn down, and the specially constructed lifting and mounting trolley was dismantled.

We had planned to join the concrete bars together in construction stages, proceeding horizontally using this trolley. A rolling crane on tracks, the size of the building cross-section, was to lift the horizontal and vertical bars, row by row, into the right position, and they would then be "threaded" together through their intersection points on steel rods. At the end of this montage process—all the bars lined up and temporarily held in place—we had planned to tension the steel cables running through the intersections and then cast the junction points. For this purpose our civil engineer Jürg Buchli had developed a special gusset in which a metal star would be embedded.
We had tested the performance of the staves and the gussets on full-scale models.
This idea of erecting a structure made of identical bars, and fitting it together in a sequence of bar-gap-bar, not proceeding vertically from the bottom up but building it like a tunnel, in linear fashion, approached the limits of conventional construction—and also the limits of what was doable in Berlin at that time.

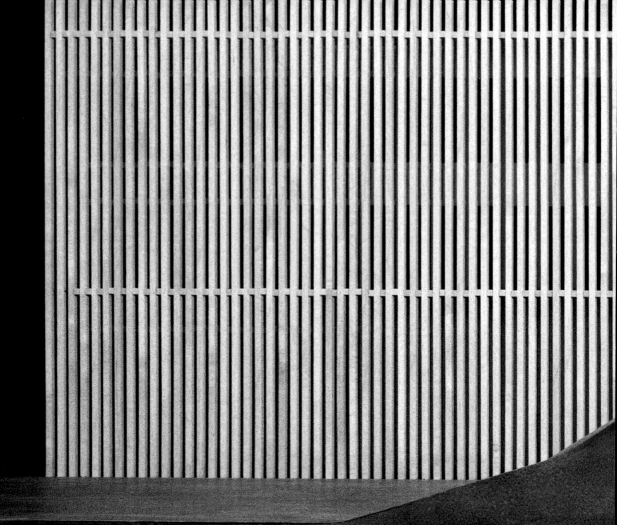

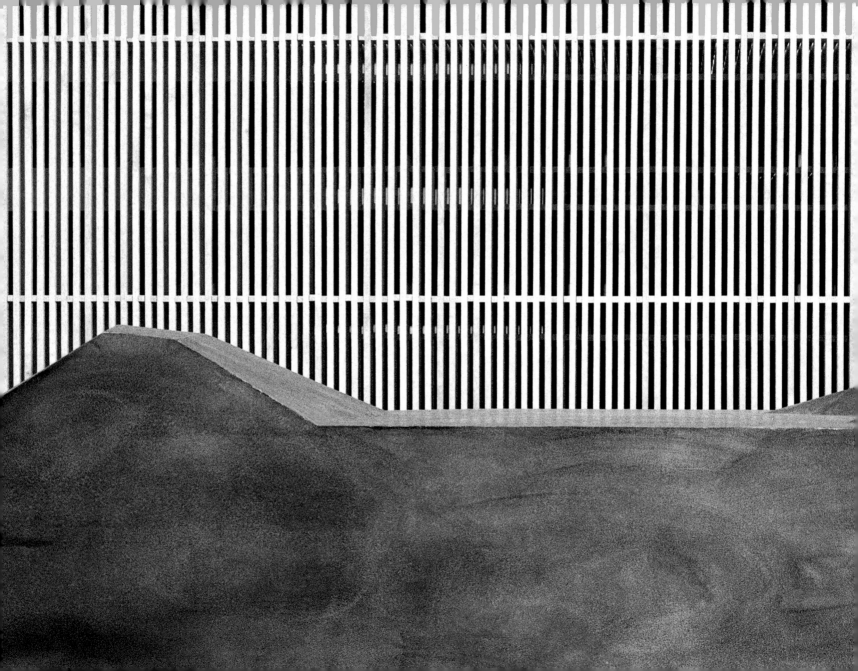

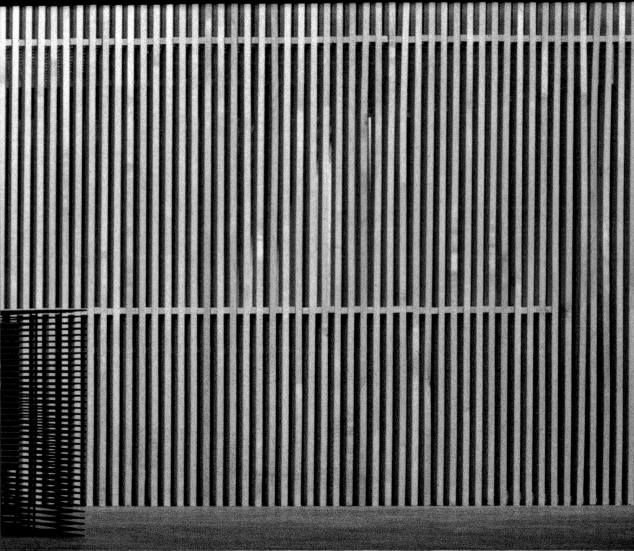

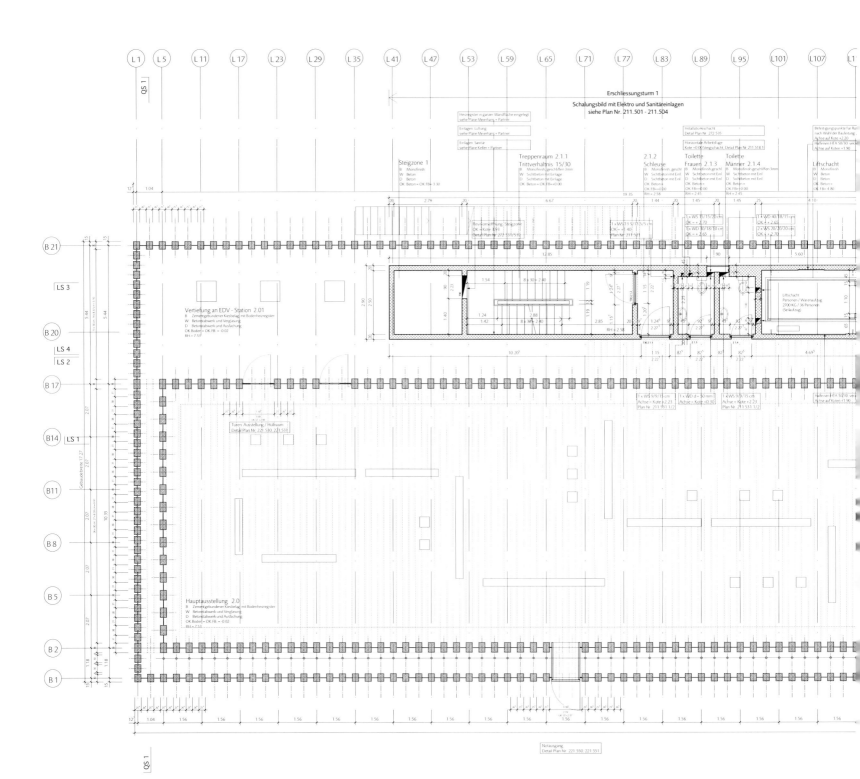

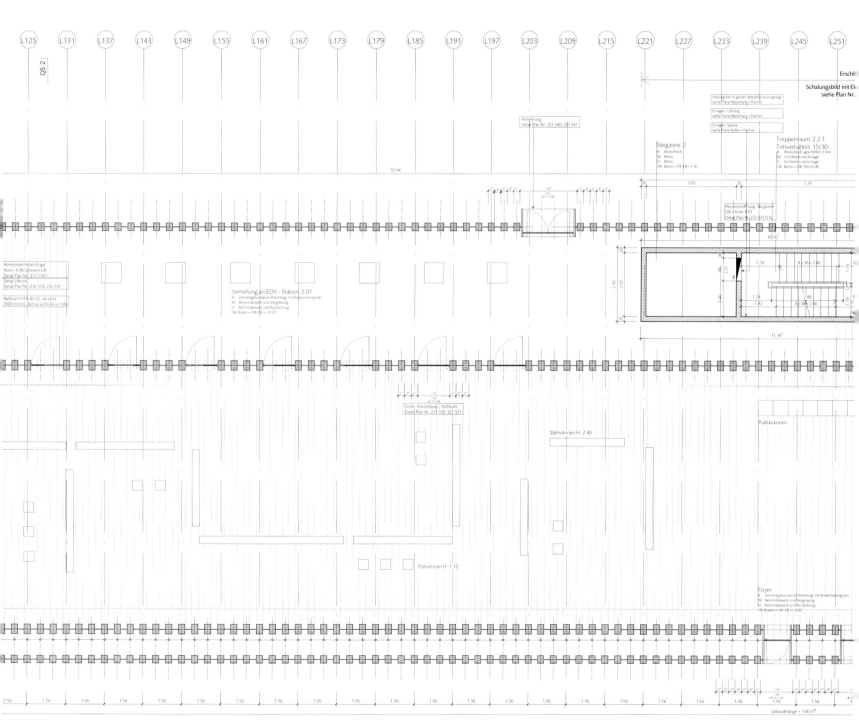

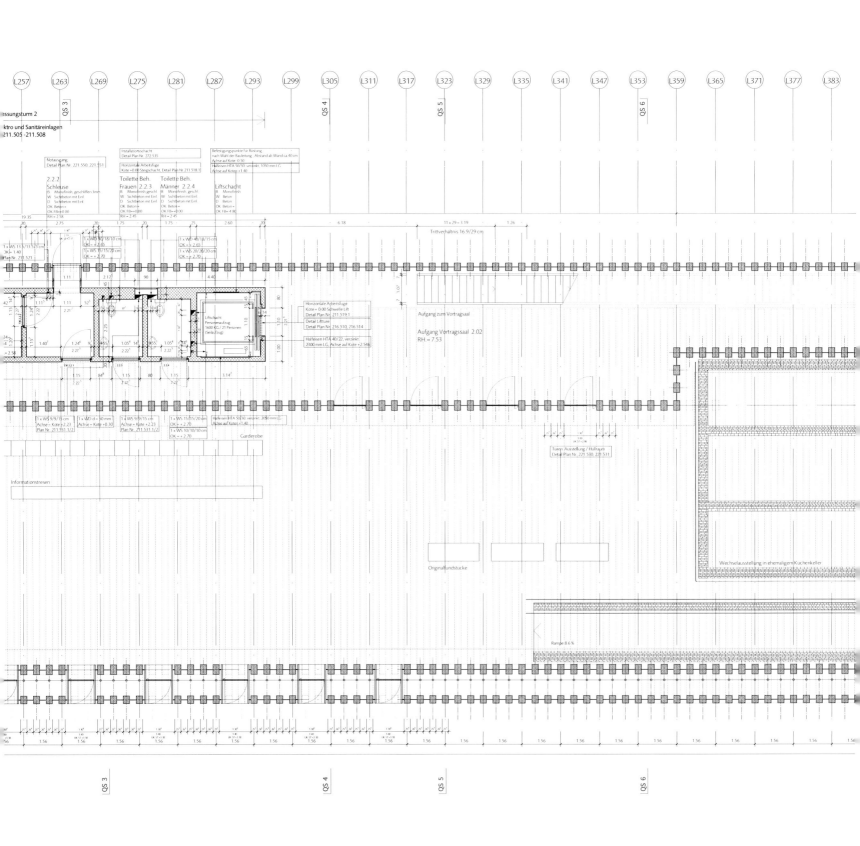

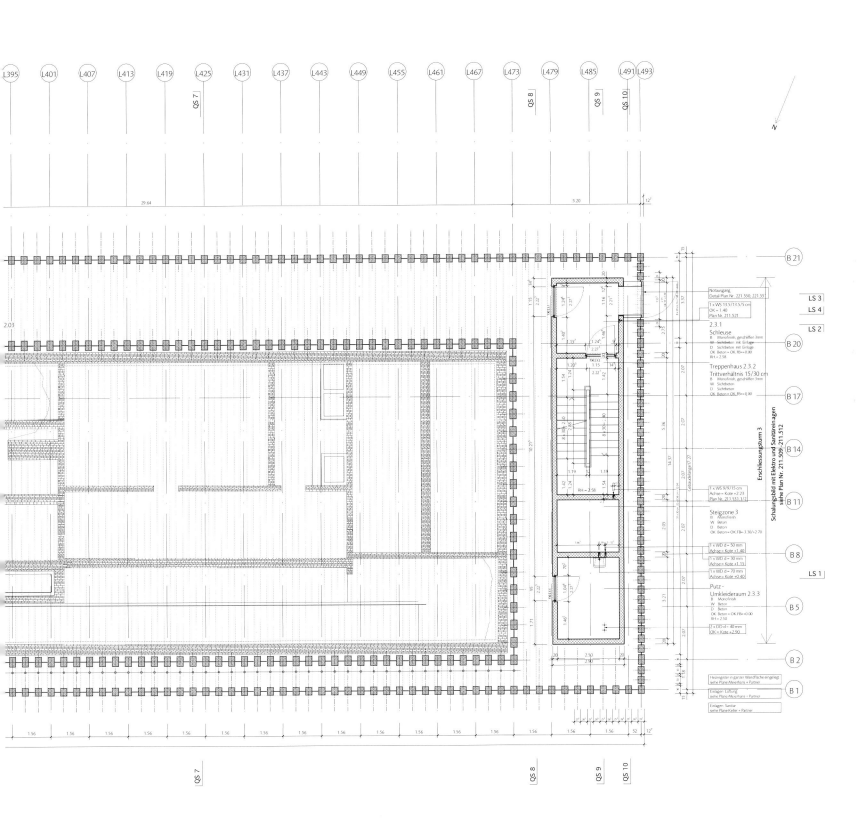

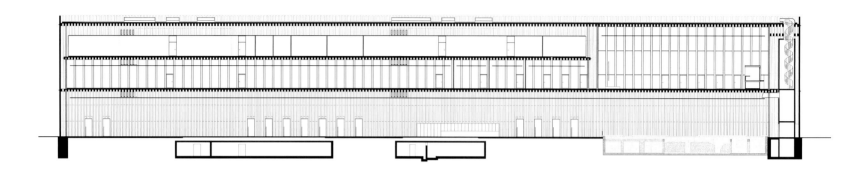
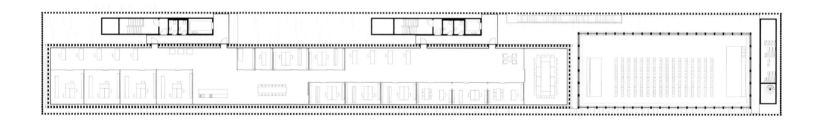
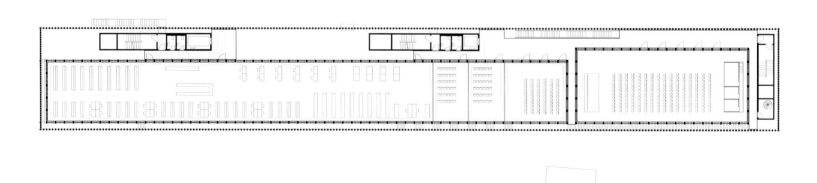

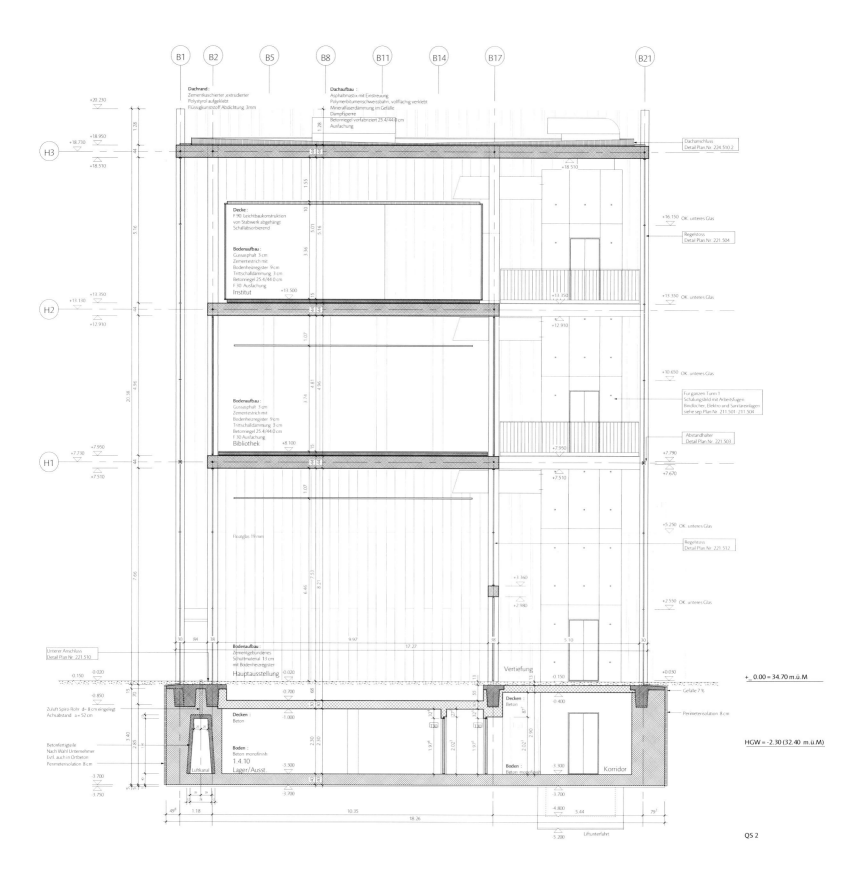

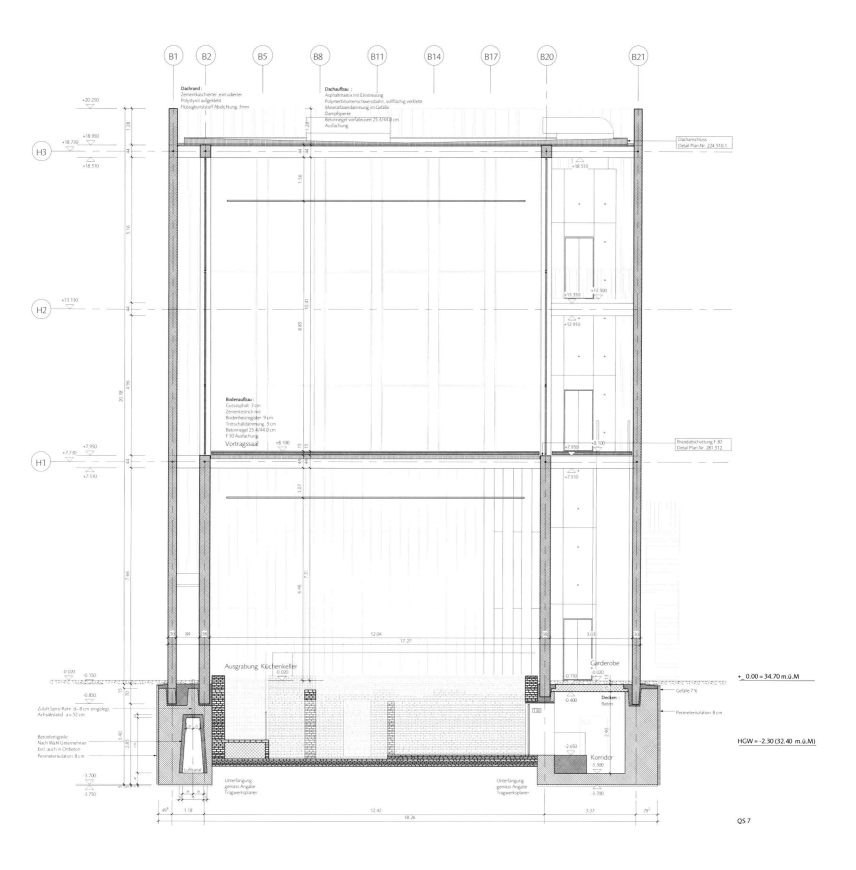

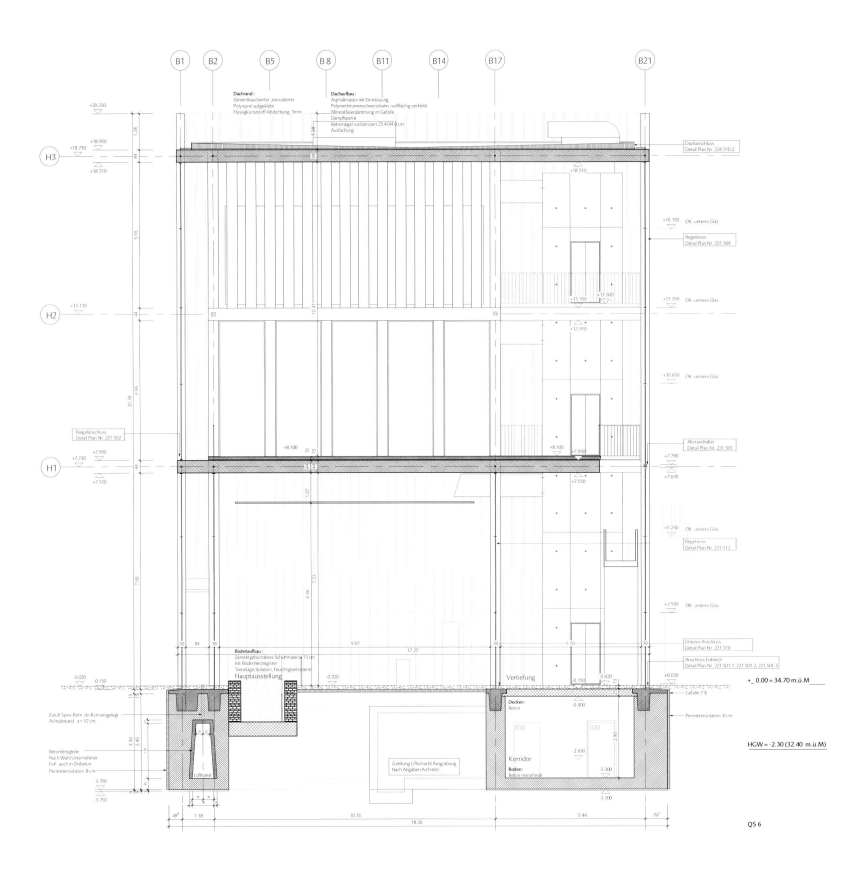

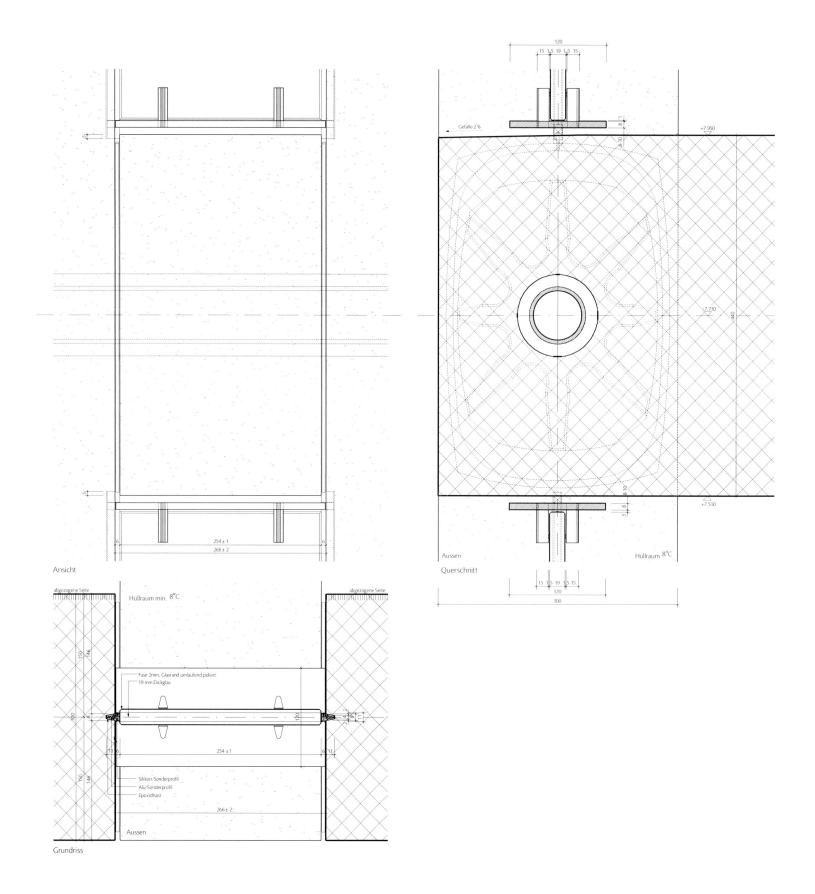

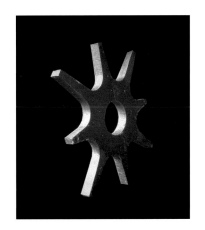

Herz Jesu Church, Munich, Germany
1996

We wanted to generate an intense, concentrated atmosphere in the church. We dreamed of a special interior encased in shells of brickwork and layers of space, a blue space ending in points of light, in a starry sky. Hollow shapes looking like upside-down stalactites of blue light would form the ceiling. The structure of this ceiling would make the space appear to extend upward forever, dissolving into infinity—that was what we hoped.

Many years later I had the chance to build a space of this kind, a space that is simultaneously open and closed to the sky, or rather, I should say, that is imbued with the wish to embody the tension between below and above, dark and bright, earth and light, protection and exposure in vibrant lightness and darkness. When I was working on the Bruder Klaus Chapel in the Eifel region, I never even thought of my old design for the Herz Jesu Church in Munich. But now, looking back, I see the affinity between the two. With the design for the church in Munich the color blue came to be a part of it; we wanted to create a blue space, an ecstatic flickering blue: we thought of blue as pure color, as material and substance transformed into light.

I never got to see the blue space of the Herz Jesu Church. I never even saw the model. It was shattered on the way from the Spanish model-builder to the jury in Munich.

On the meaning of the color blue, which made such an impression on me in the Giotto chapel in Padua or in the paintings of Yves Klein: the man who was to become Abbot Daniel, for whose Benedictine community I was able to build the Sogn Benedetg Chapel, told me that blue is connected with the divine and with divine truth. For the early Church Fathers, blue symbolizes the wish for a connection with heaven, and Jesus, he wrote me, wore a blue garment for the three years of his preaching. Only later did I fall in love with Antonello da Messina's *Virgin Annunciate*, who wears this wonderful blue mantle.

At about the same time, we also addressed the theme of color as light in a red color space that we designed for the Poetic Landscape project in Bad Salzuflen. It, too, remained an idea and a dream.

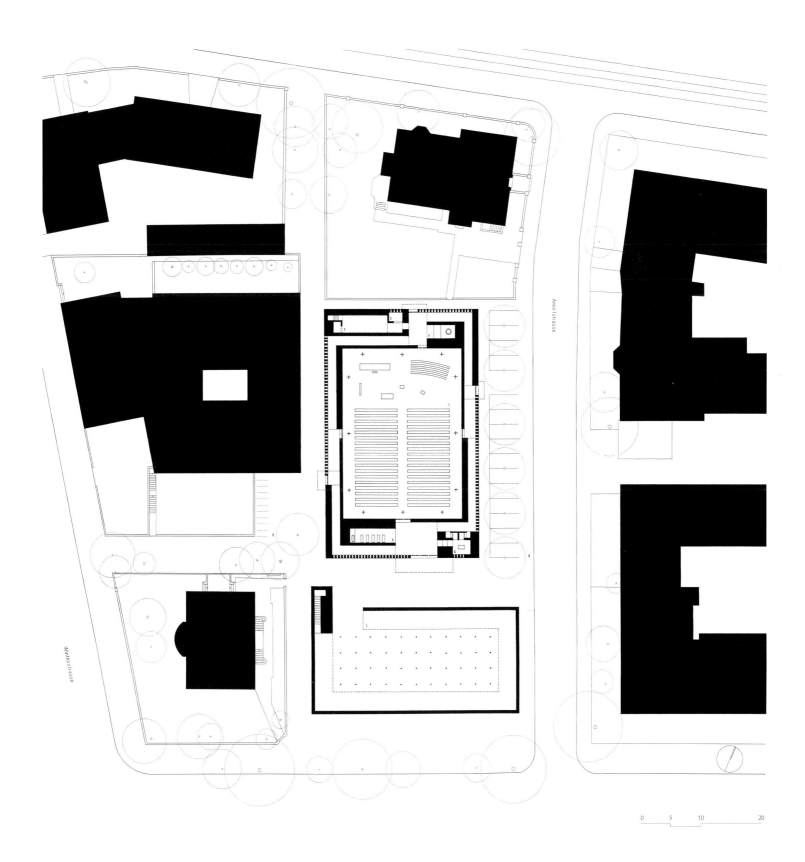

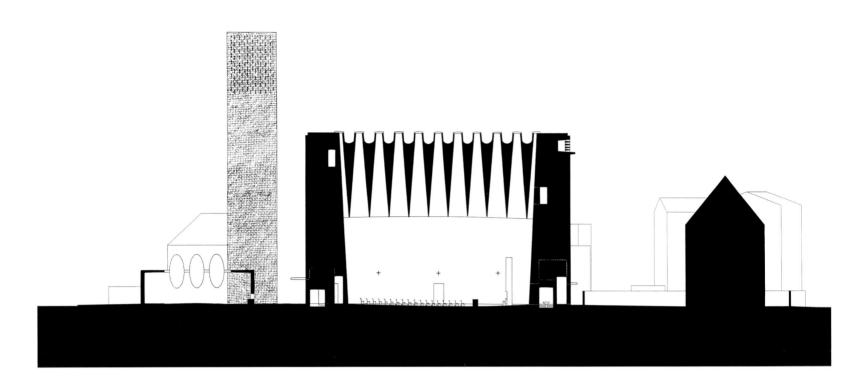
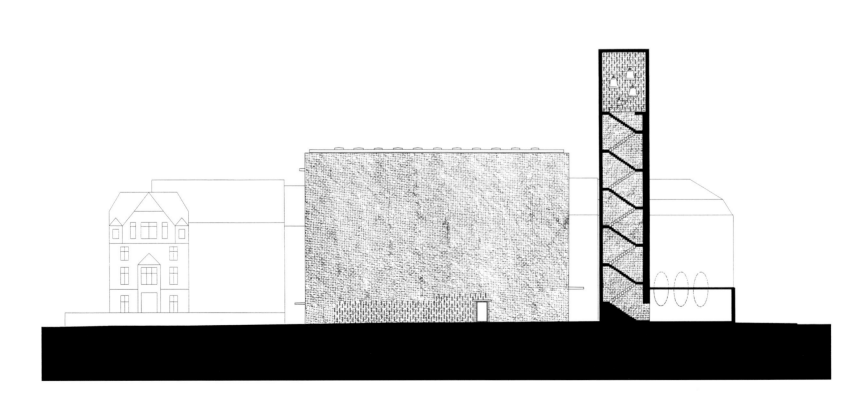

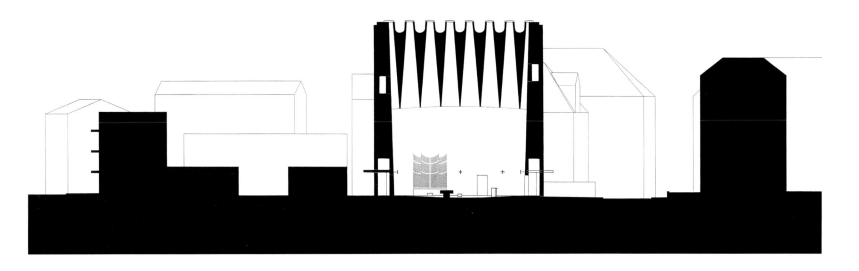

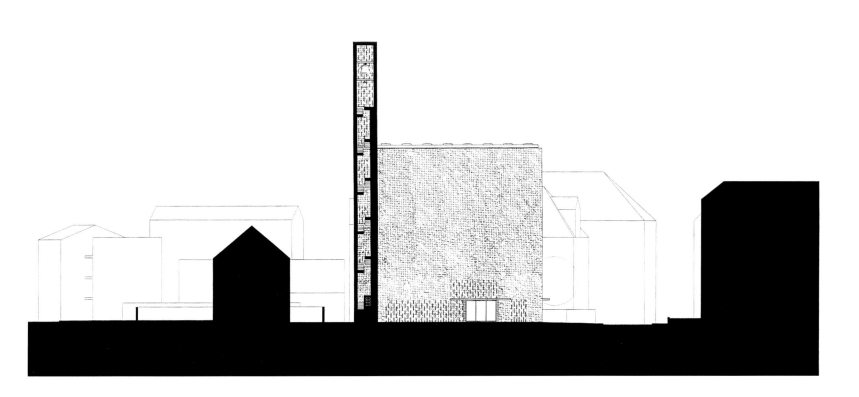

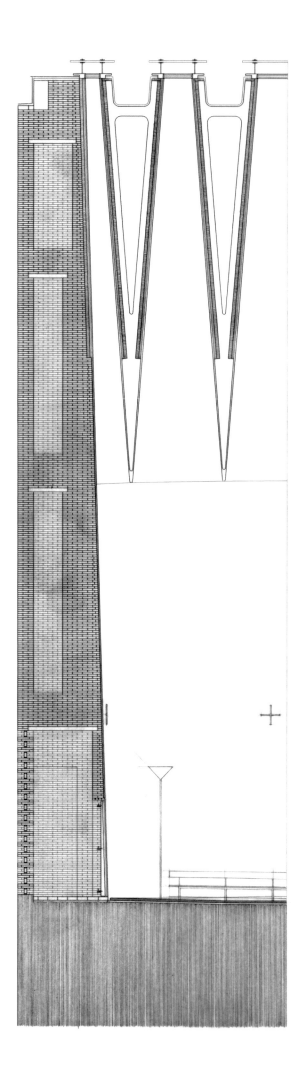

Laban Centre for Movement and Dance, London, England
1997

The basic idea of the design was to inscribe a tower for dance in the city silhouette: dance studios stacked vertically, rooms of various sizes and shapes, different views and lighting situations, a sculpture of spatial vessels, platforms, and compartments, encased in a transparent membrane.

The life inside the Laban Centre for Movement and Dance in London is displayed in the transparent and yet opaque cladding of the building. Seen from outside, it looks like a performance that is constantly changing.

I well remember being impressed by the unpretentious, industrial-commercial atmosphere of the proposed site on Deptford Creek. Despite its extravagant expressivity, I think the design reflects the atmosphere of the place well.

Even today I like to imagine the work, the coming and going of the dancers and teachers, which my sketches of the dance-tower on the water seem to be celebrating.

Swiss Sound Box, Swiss Pavilion, Expo 2000,
Hanover, Germany
1997–2000

I write this text now in 2013, at a time when many firms, institutions, nations, and people carefully groom their public image, putting on a mask so they will be seen as they want to be seen and not as they actually are. In this context I am more amazed than ever that, back in the year 2000, we Swiss chose to make our presentation at the World Exhibition in Hanover a *Gesamtkunstwerk*. Our theme was not self-presentation, but hospitality. We were offering a place to relax away from the noise of the fair; we made music, we ran three bars with snacks and drinks. Our gamble paid off. The Swiss Sound Box pavilion was a "re-sounding" success.

The Swiss Federal Government, our client, wanted us to use as much indigenous wood as possible and to build sustainably. So in this non-place in the fairground, we set up a huge stack of wood. We brought to Hanover around three thousand cubic meters of freshly cut fir and larch wood from Switzerland and stacked it up in layers to dry out, as they used to do in lumberyards where the planks dried in the air. Our civil engineer Jürg Conzett helped me develop a tensioning system that enabled us to press the wooden construction down onto the ground. The freshly cut, still wet wood could dry out and settle, without the construction becoming unstable. In the six months the exhibition was up we had to adjust the tension only once with the device we made for this purpose to restore the proper pressure on the beams as they settled down.

We tensioned the stacked wood walls with steel rods and pressed them down onto the ground; the smoothly planed beams were not damaged at all, for our plan at the end of the exhibition was to carefully dismantle them and sell them as air-dried lumber.

The natural properties of wood were a great advantage in the pavilion. When it was hot out on the fairground, it was pleasantly cool between the wooden walls, and as it slowly got colder in the fall, the open wooden structure gave a feeling of warmth.

The stacks of wood were arranged to form a kind of labyrinth in which visitors would discover little spatial events, like clearings in the forest, offering moments of rest and relaxation. Even after multiple visits, it was hard to tell whether you had yet seen the whole pavilion, and this gave the structure a special appeal despite its relatively small size. On the other hand, in the confusing maze of joined spaces there was only one nine-square-foot spot without a direct view out into the open, so, despite the labyrinthine character of the stacked structure, it retained a pleasant feeling of freedom and clear orientation.

The artistic concept of a pavilion with a musical composition at its center which, performed by almost five hundred musicians, ran for six months and was constantly changing, emerged in collaboration with composer Daniel Ott, literary theorist Plinio Bachmann, dramaturge Karoline Gruber, fashion designer Ida Gut, and gastronome Max Rigendinger. It is described in the book *Swiss Sound Box* (Basel, 2000).

At the end of the exhibition the Swiss Federation sold all the lumber as planned. It was used for park benches, flooring, wall paneling, furniture, doors, houses, and for the dome at CERN in Geneva.

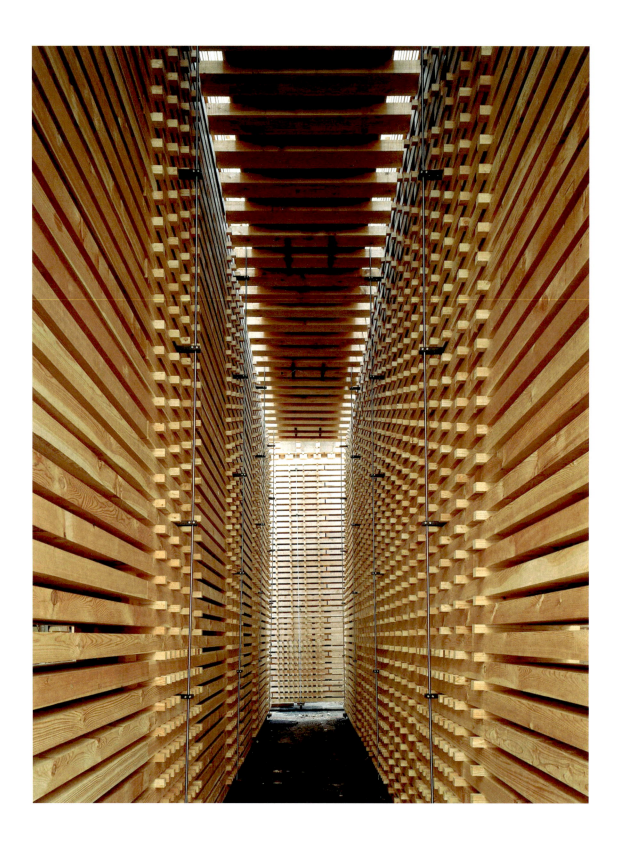

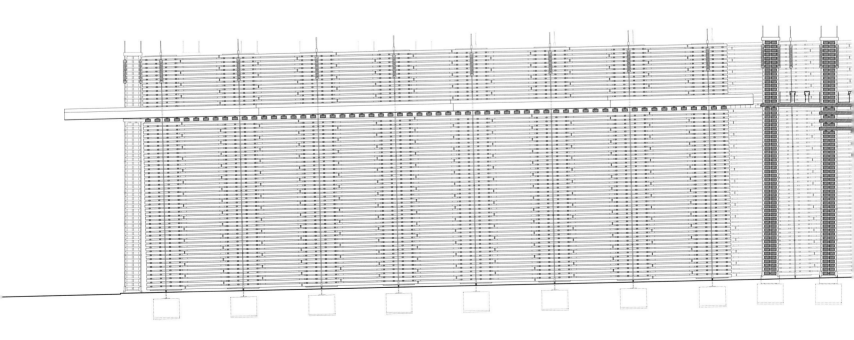

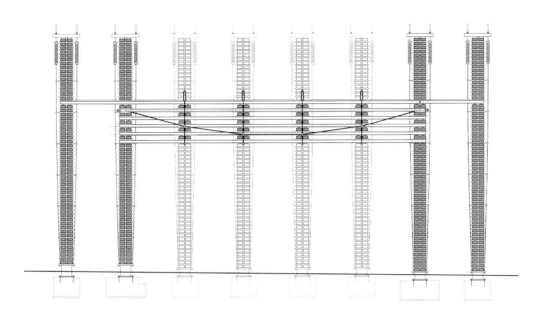

0 1 2   5

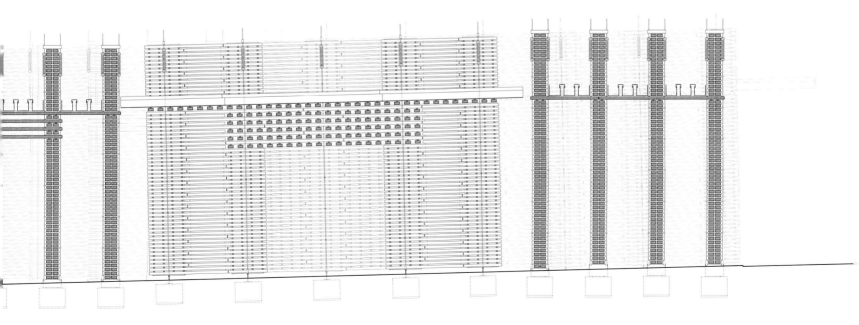

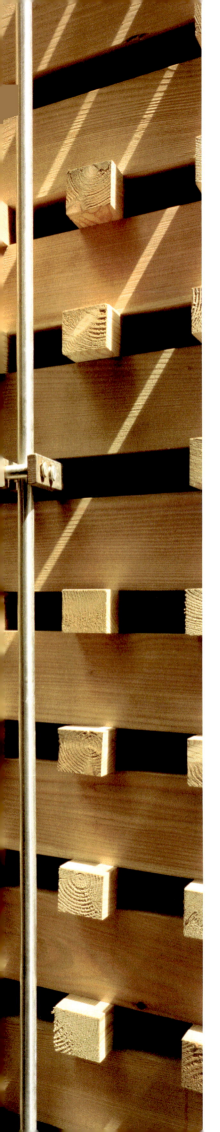

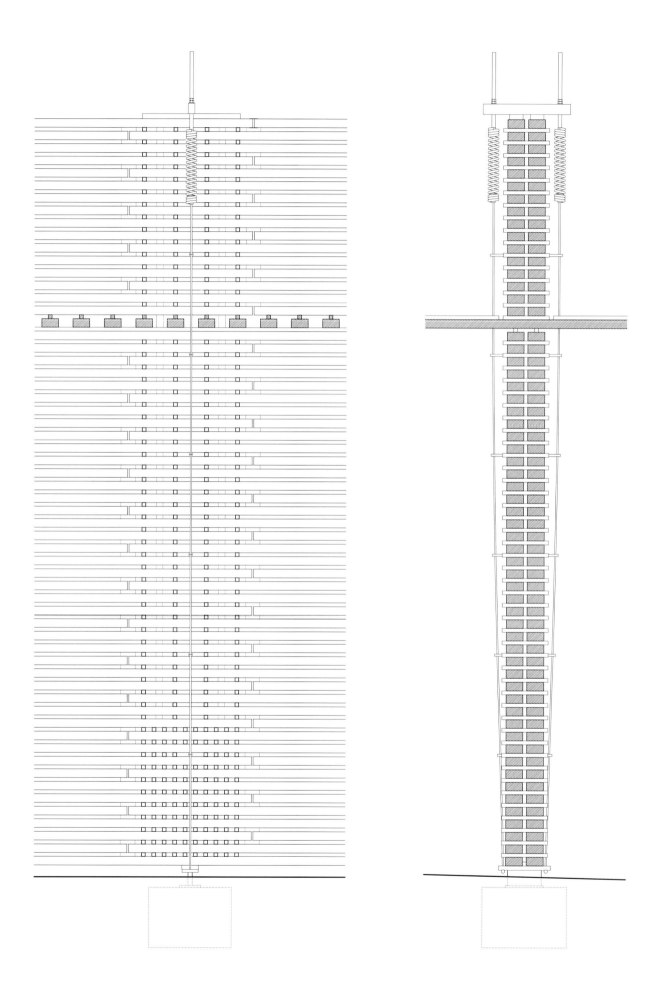

Luzi House, Jenaz, Graubünden
1997–2002

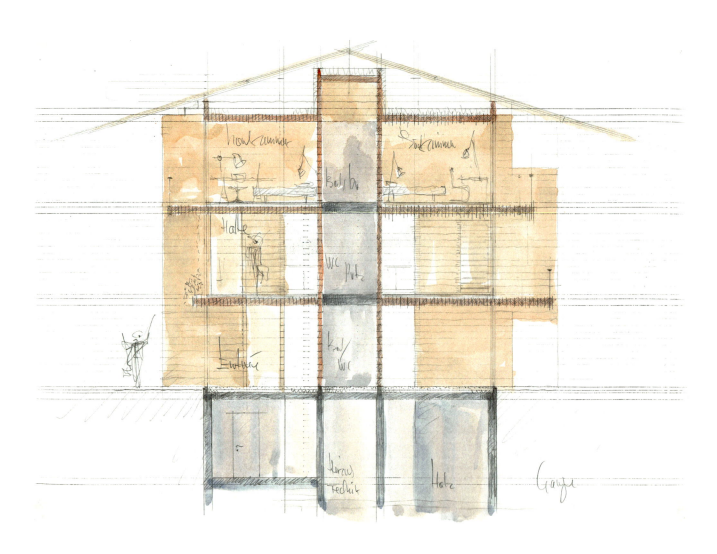

The clients, Valentin and Lilian Luzi, wanted a large home in Jenaz for themselves and their six children. It was to be spacious, it was to be bright, and built out of solid wood: these were their wishes.

Living in a blockhouse of solid wood has a special quality which is felt both in its aura and in the physical experience of living there. As opposed to stone or concrete, logs do not draw off warmth from the human body, and thus even in cold weather they feel warm. Conversely, when it is warm or hot, the wooden beams do not radiate previously absorbed heat as stone or metal would, and so their effect is actually cooling. To get this effect in a room requires that it be built of solid beams. If the wood is reduced to ordinary board thickness, the climatic advantage is lost. The more these advantages became clear to me, the more willing I was to look for new solutions for this type of solid construction. The Luzi House ushered in a small research project on this subject, later pursued in the houses in Leis.

Blockhouses made of heavy logs are problematic in that the stacked wooden beams of the walls dry out through the years and settle, so that the walls start slanting, as frequently seen in old buildings in which the stone foundations are not all on a single level. Stairs, doors, and windows, moreover, have to be made in such a way that they do not suffer structural damage when the walls of the building settle as they dry. In the first few years this amounts to about three centimeters per floor. In time, as the wood dries out, it stops moving.

A further difficulty in building traditional blockhouses is the desire for ever larger windows. The construction of a blockhouse, known here as *Strickbau*, is in principle based on four tree-length sized walls made of stacked beams fitted together into a quadrilateral spatial unit, a rigid "wooden box." If the openings cut into the walls of the box are too large, they diminish the stability of the wooden walls: they start to come apart, and the areas around the window need to be reinforced in unattractive ways.

We found our answer to the large window question while working on the Luzi House. We constructed five small, freestanding "binder" towers to act as hollow, load-bearing buttresses; these are tied together by ceiling panels. Into this support structure, we cut chink-like windows to admit some light. The large spaces between the towers have glass walls and accommodate the living and sleeping areas of the house. The towers themselves contain ancillary spaces. The clients liked my idea of using these spaces to access each of the four bedrooms on the top floor directly via a separate staircase from the lower living level. This creates individuality, while the proximity of the bedrooms to the family areas ensures a charming intimacy. The layout of the house celebrates the view onto the countryside with four different landscape pictures for four living spaces on all three levels.

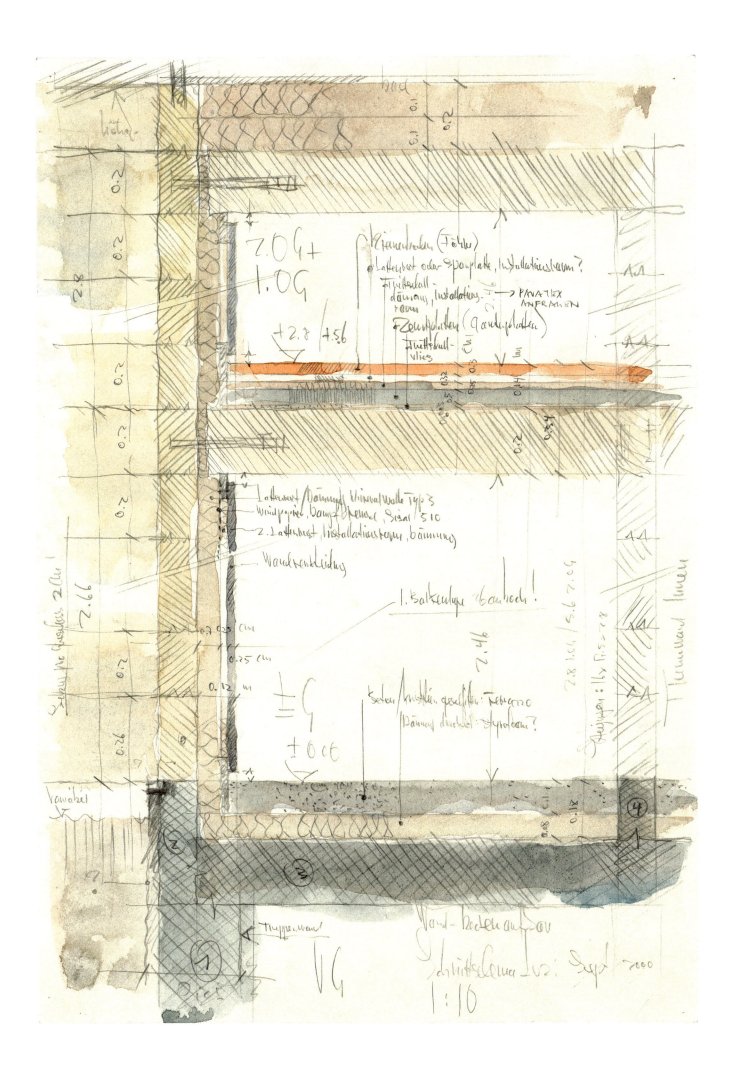

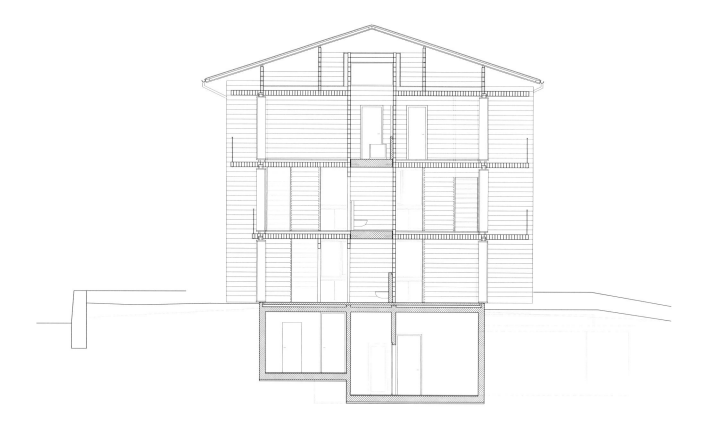

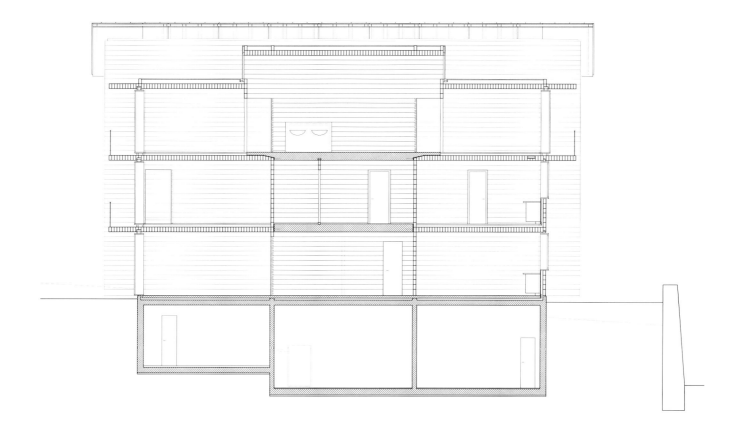

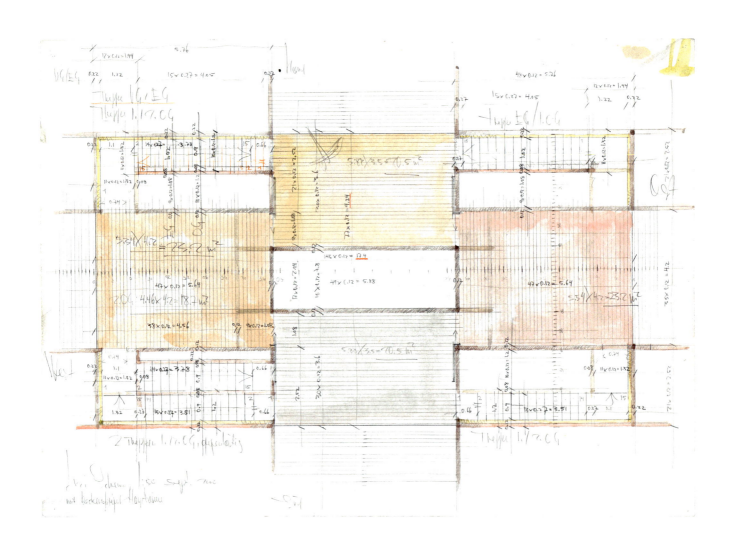

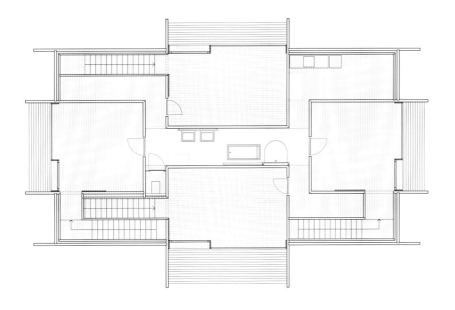
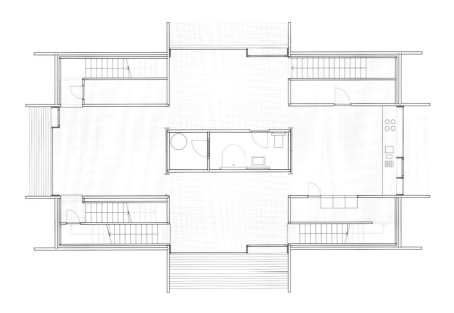
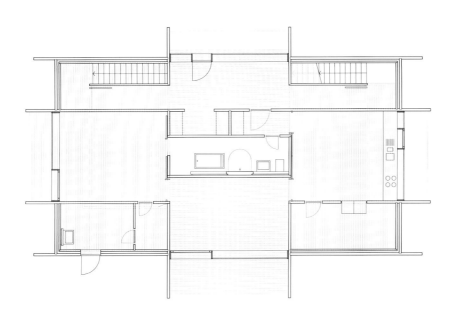

Kolumba Art Museum, Cologne, Germany
1997–2007

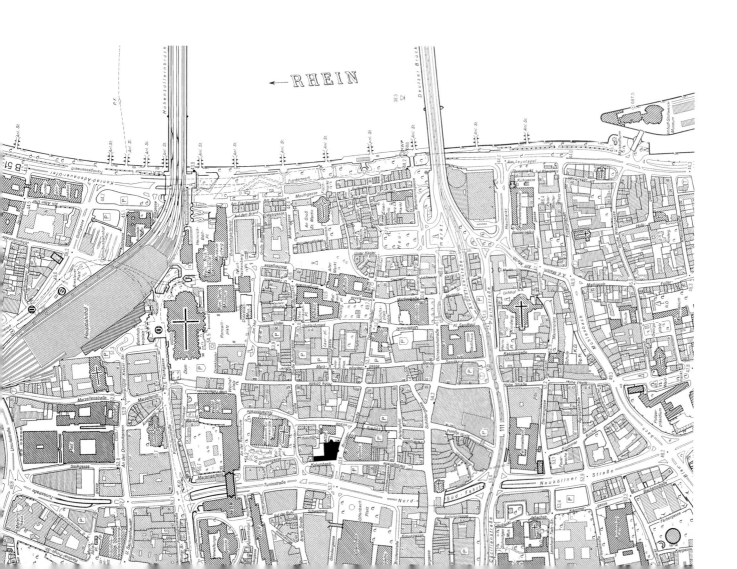

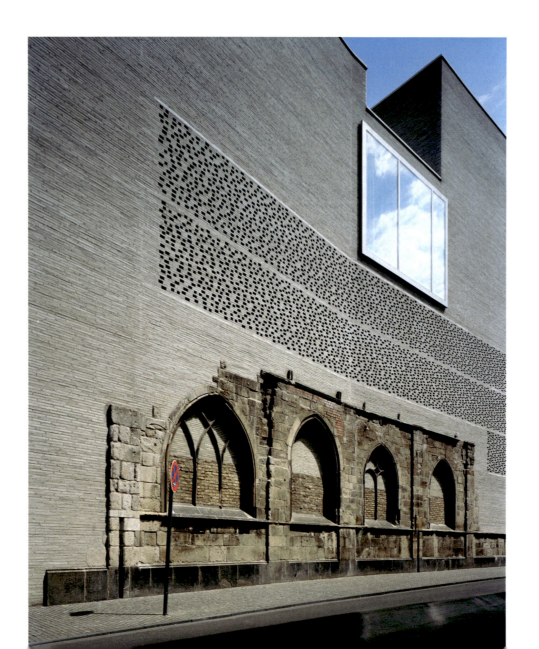

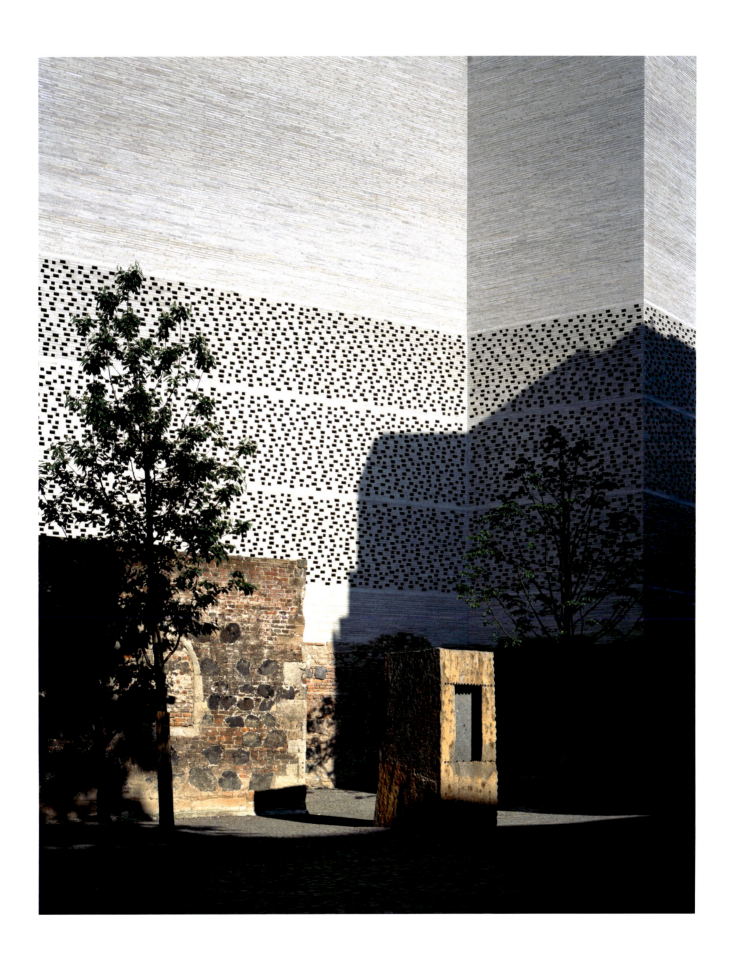

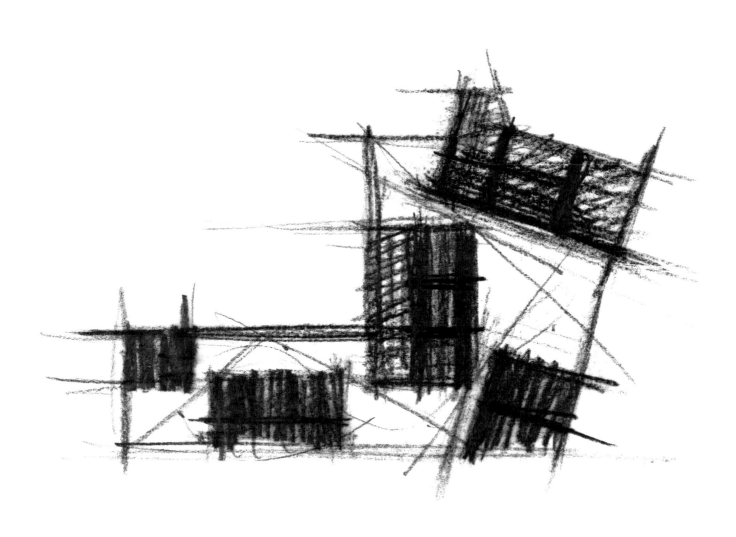

We had never expected to win the competition to build a new art museum in the center of Cologne on the site of the Church of St. Columba, which was bombed out in the Second World War. At the time, architects generally held the opinion that new construction should present as great a contrast as possible to old buildings. As a rule, they responded to massive old walls by designing lighter constructions of steel and glass. But the jury liked our impulse for an older-style architectural stance that would bring old and new together in a new whole geared toward harmony rather than contrast.

Our design for Cologne respects what remains of the church, and leaves it in view. In putting up the new construction we did not remove a single stone from the ruins. Our building material was brick; this was the material used for the first repairs made after the destruction of the war, and we found it as a lining around the old church windows and as a temporary covering for the broken-off capstones. We also knew that brick has a long tradition in the area, including the buildings by Rudolf Schwarz from the middle of the last century. The Danish brickmaker Christian Petersen was able to manufacture a new, slimmer brick for us, which allowed us to make a good join with the Gothic tracery work and the broken-off butts of the walls, and to build up on top of the old walls. These "Kolumba bricks," as they are now called, have a shape that reminds us of Roman bricks. We used them to build the openwork, double-layered outer wall, permeable to light and air, which surrounds the excavated space of the lost Church of St. Columba and forms the massive sheathing of the museum.

Civil engineer Jürg Buchli helped us construct this wall without expansion joints and made sure that the old walls could bear some of the load of the new walls built on top of them.

The new building evolved from the foundations of the original church. We followed the late Gothic footprint exactly and expanded it to take advantage of an adjoining empty lot on Kolumbastrasse. Thus the shape of the new museum not only speaks of its contents as a museum of art, but also reflects to a high degree its historic origins.

Kolumba is a time machine. This must have been clear to the then officials of the archdiocese, Norbert Feldhoff, Joachim Plotzek, Josef Rüenauver, and Cardinal Meisner, when they chose St. Columba's Church as the site for their new museum: a bombed-out late Gothic church, with the earth floor inside removed and the original foundations exposed layer by layer down to the remains of Roman walls; church ruins in which Gottfried Böhm built a little chapel after the war for the "Madonna in the Rubble," the statue that had miraculously survived intact. A place with such a profound historical aura was predestined to become an art museum. This assignment was everything at once: unique, seductive, and challenging. It was an ongoing project with us for ten years. There was joy in the shared ideas at the start and at the ground-breaking, there were the difficulties of engineering and building the project, and there was the pleasure of success which outshone all that had gone before.

The work on Kolumba had the intimate feeling of a family venture. In considering, designing, and building the project we did not have the sense that our client was an institution, waiting for results to study and judge, but rather it was a group of like-minded colleagues who took part in the process of creating the building and had a conscious influence on its development. I love this kind of collaboration, which I sometimes feel is lacking when clients are interested in results only and not in the process of shaping the outcome. Nowhere else have we been able to create a spatial organism out of historical remains as we have here with the Kolumba Museum. The curators' only specification was that it contain a rich variety of exhibition spaces in different shapes, sizes, and light qualities in which the pieces of the collection would in time come to find their natural homes.

This gave rise to a walkway that tours the museum starting on Kolumbastrasse, turning briefly into the main mass of the new space, and then, after an initial twist, opening up to face the new courtyard space with its pebble paving, tall trees-of-heaven, and bench with Hans Josephsohn's sculpture of a reclining female figure, before moving back into the main space of the building and ascending in ever greater sweeping curves to the level of the main floor. Here, in the central space over the old church, the tour comes to an end, surrounded by three pairs of rooms which each terminate in tower-like spaces to the north, east, and south.

This tour through the museum is also a path from the historical ruins at ground level up towards the light and the view. Gradually windows appear along the way, letting daylight warmly illuminate the clay-plaster coating of the walls: we look out into the city, along with the quietly smiling seventeenth-century Madonna and Child at the end of the first long stairway.

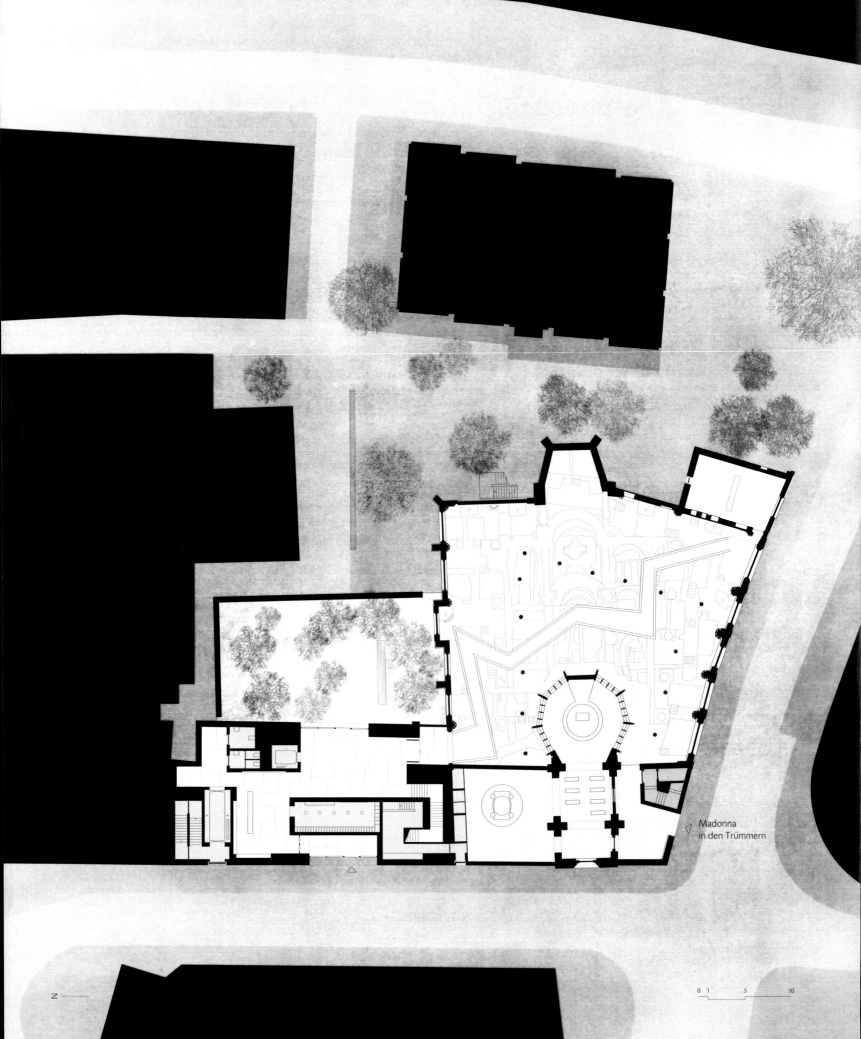

Madonna in den Trümmern

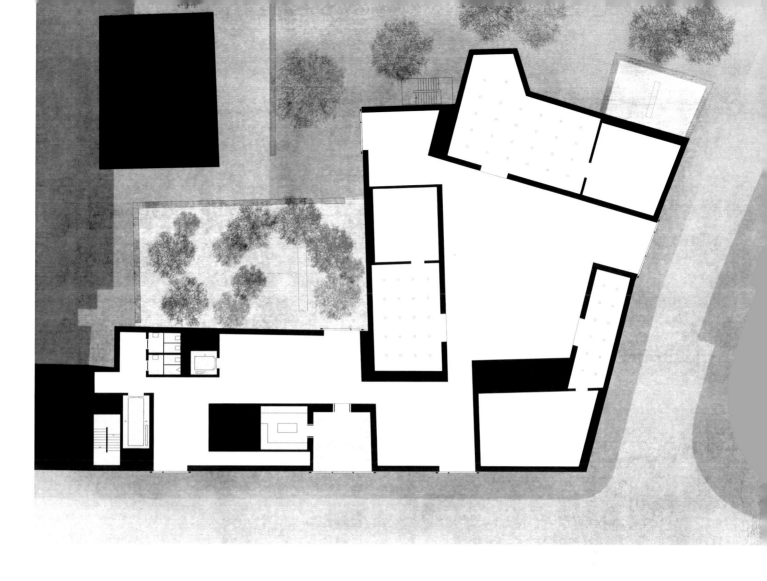
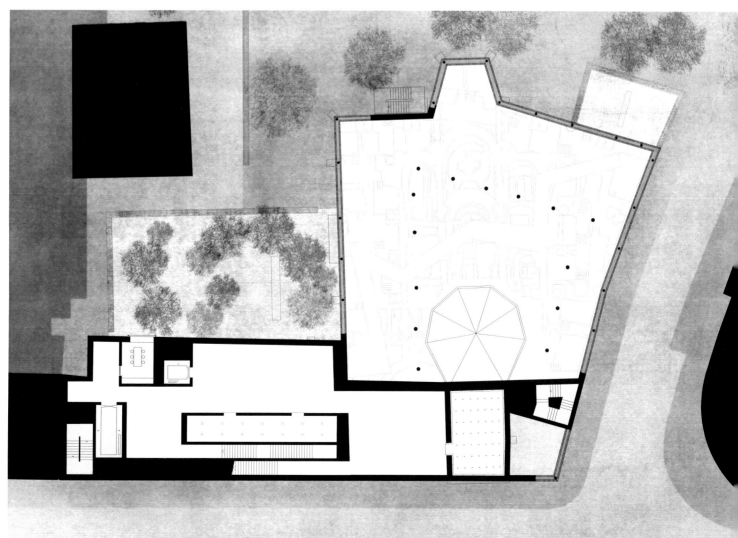

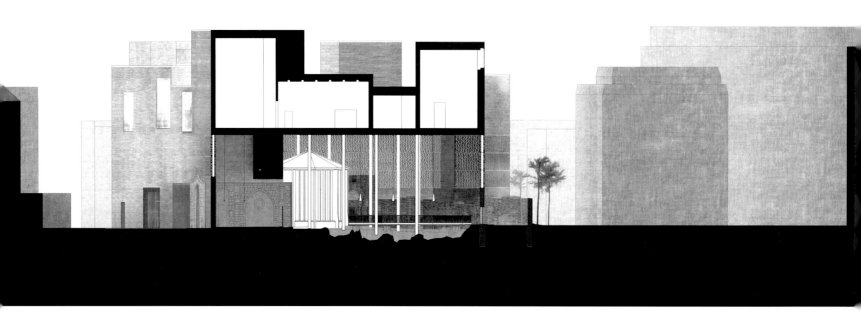

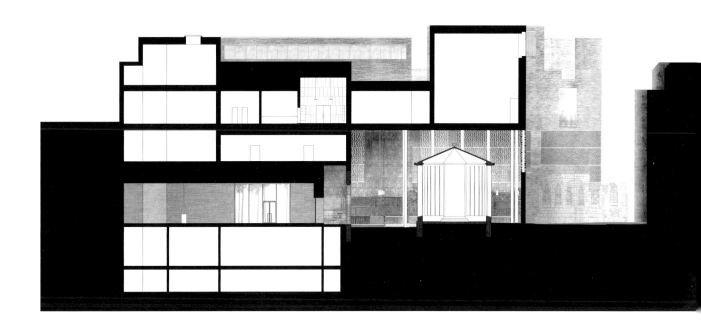

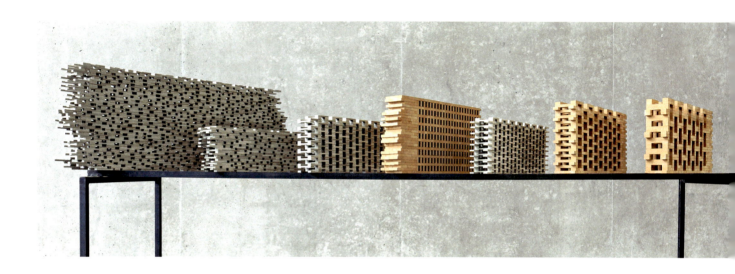